Torry - its History an
by
Gordon Bathgate

Fore Close© Aberdeen Journals

Girdleness Publishing

49 Girdleness Road
Torry, Aberdeen
Scotland, UK
AB11 8DG
email: girdlenessbooks@aol.com

Printed in The UK

Published by

Girdleness Publishing

Old Torry © Aberdeen Library and Information Services

Copyright © Gordon Bathgate 2006
Cover design by - David Wilson

ISBN 0-9554234-0-6
ISBN 978-0-9554234-0-6

1
Old Torry

As I reached the cairn at the top of Tullos Hill I felt like I'd reacquainted myself with an old friend. Although I view it from my bedroom window everyday this was the first time I'd been within touching distance of the obelisk in over 20 years. The reason for my trip to Tullos Hill was because of the breathtaking view of Torry it offers. This would be an ideal location to begin my book about the area that has been my home for most of my life. I paused to catch my breath and marvelled at the stunning landscape stretched out before me.

Tullos Hill is known locally as the 'Gramps' but the area has been known by many names in the past. The range of hills were often referred to as 'The Mounth' and the name still survives today in 'Cairn o' Mount'. In his famous map of 1661, Parson James Gordon called them the Grangebeen Hills. While in his "Book of St. Fittick", published in 1901, Dr. Thomas White Ogilvie describes Tullos Hill in colourful fashion.

> *"A miniature mountain chain in itself, studded with hillocks which are its outliers, and cairns which are its peaks, and for tarns and lochs the little water-filled hollows choked with water sedge and cinquefoil, and carpeted around their swampy margins with the green and crimson plush of bogmoss and sundew, a carpet spangled with the orange stars of the bog asphodel, and beyond that the heather and whin, blazing in bloom of gold in spring, dark green, and purple in the fall, whilst a strip of woodland yields a succession of greens throughout the year".*

Nowadays they form part of the area known officially as Loirston Country Park and are in fact the most easterly ridges of the Grampian Mountains. If you stand at the highest point and look northwards, you may experience a sense of what the old village was like centuries ago. Below Tullos Hill lies the Vale of Tullos and beyond that is Torry Hill. Very little remains of the old landscape and it's hard to believe the urban sprawl that dominates the view was once little more than a few agricultural settlements dotted around Torry Hill. The fields stretched from the Bay of Nigg in the east, to the River Dee in the west. Westwards, a vast wooded area stretched out along the steep slopes of the river's edge. Remnants of the "Lover's Wood" still exist today at Craiginches.

Here again, in this extract from the "Book of St. Fittick", Dr. Thomas White Ogilvie describes what the scene looked like in his day. With his usual flair for vivid prose he wrote: -

> *"It is full of quiet charm, this little glen, with its Kirk on the height and its Kirk in the hollow, extending from the great gap in the cliff, which forms the Bay, up to the river, where, with majestic bend, it sweeps glittering and gurgling by Allenvale and Duthie Park, sweetest of resting places for the quick and the dead".*

To the east of the "Gramps" there is a rocky headland called Gregness, the southern tip of the Bay of Nigg. At the north tip of the Bay of Nigg is the rock-strewn promontory of Girdleness, which gives the lighthouse its name. This area remains largely unaffected by urbanisation and still looks much the same as it did centuries ago. The area between Girdleness and the South Breakwater is called Greyhope Bay. Greyhope is an English corruption of the Gaelic 'Creg Hop', meaning rocky bay.

From Greyhope Bay looking north, you can see the harbour channel, the North Pier, the harbour and Aberdeen beach. The land around the coast originally stretched several hundred yards further out to sea than it does now but erosion has caused it to disappear under water. The harbour area has also undergone significant changes. Before the North Pier was built, there was a low, wind-swept sand dune called the Sandness. The village of Footdee stood further west by the waterside, near to where St. Clement's Church now stands.

The land to the north of the river would also have looked very different as recently as 150 years ago. Before then the land between what is now the North Esplanade and Guild Street was a soggy mess of little tributaries subject to seasonal flooding. The Dee's channel was artificially diverted during the mid 19th century and a sizeable area of marshlands was recovered for development.

Torry lies on a plateau of rock infused with moraine and granite that could only have come from Deeside, via river or glacier action. Variations in the sub-Arctic climate would have caused ice to ebb and flow across North East Scotland several times. During the last main glacial advance known as the Devensian, the ice sheet would have covered the Torry area. When the Pleistocene period ended 12,000 years ago the ice receded westwards leaving a large melt water channel between Torry and Tullos Hills.

Opinions about the geological origins of the area differ wildly. Several geologists opine that during the Ice Age the Dee Glacier flowed into the North Sea at two points leaving Torry Hill as an island between them. They believe the river split at the point that is now the Duthie Park. One flowed along the Tullos Valley and entered at the Bay of Nigg and the other followed another course to the north. A layer of silt gradually built up and blocked the river's southern exit, causing the river to follow the deeper northern channel. The supporters of this theory cite the marshland in the Vale of Tullos as an indication of the river's former course.

However other geologists doubt the Dee ever flowed down the Vale of Tullos and they offer a different explanation for the marshland. Their belief is that around 6000 years ago, sea levels rose and flooded into the Vale of Tullos. A bar of sediment built up forming a coastal lagoon in the valley. When the lagoon eventually receded it left a quagmire at the bottom of the hollow. The Tullos Burn, which flows into the Bay, is really a drainage ditch dug centuries ago in an effort to make the marshy land drier. The swamp area was completely drained during the last two decades and now forms part of St. Fittick's Park.

The first humans arrived at the Bay Of Nigg during the Middle Stone Age period. These pioneers tended to stick close to the shoreline and roam from settlement to settlement. These drifters didn't build permanent dwellings and preferred to use tents made from animal skins. Around 3000 BC, Man abandoned his nomadic existence and began to cultivate crops and keep animals. There is evidence of primitive agricultural settlements in the Vale of Tullos.

During the Bronze Age the "Beaker Folk" arrived in the area. They were known as the Beaker Folk because of their custom of placing a clay container or urn alongside their dead. These people adapted to the local environment and pioneered the use of metals. They are widely regarded as the original ancestors of the local population.

For many years Tullos Hill was a range of hillocks covered in trees and bramble bushes. A variety of Oak, Pine and Birch Trees were planted all over the range in 1799 and continued to flourish until the early 1900s. David Morrice, the owner of Tullos House, was responsible for the plantation. Morrice had purchased the lands of Middleton, Altens and Tullos from the Council for £42 8s in 1786.

Although the area has been progressively encroached by urban development in recent years it still contains a few clues to the past. Several consumption dykes are still in existence. These wide stone erections are so called because they consumed stones from the fields during agricultural improvements and land reclamation.

The hill contains four excellent examples of the Beaker Folk's Bronze Age Burial Cairns. Each cairn marks the peaks of the hill range. The pinnacle is marked by the Baron's Cairn with two smaller ones on opposite ends of the hill. At the west is the Cat's Cairn while the Crab's Cairn is situated at the east. In addition, the Tullos Cairn stands below the skyline on the northern face of the hill.

Also scattered across the hillside are several smaller stone mounds that are thought to be early attempts at clearing uneven ground for agricultural purposes. These Field Clearance Cairns were discovered in 2005 when fire damage destroyed the surrounding foliage making the stacks more visible.

4

These ancient obelisks were originally built to commemorate long forgotten events but were frequently used as navigational aids by sailors and travellers. A lookout was posted at the Baron's Cairn during times of crisis to warn of approaching enemies. A large concrete slab marks the peak and makes an ideal vantage point to survey the surrounding countryside. Sadly all the cairns are now in a dilapidated state as the meticulously laid stones have long since been scattered by vandals.

Another point of interest is the Elf Hillock, an old burial mound that derives its name from an old legend. Past inhabitants of Torry believed this curious knoll was a magical place where fairies and elves met nightly to dance and socialise into the wee small hours of the morning. Despite the rampant urbanization that's taken place over the past three decades it still survives today, although you'll have to look hard to find it. It's in the wooded area at the bottom of Tullos Hill behind the business units on the industrial estate. You can gain access along a narrow tree-lined path leading from Greenbank Road.

People who settled in the area are thought to have arrived here from Central Europe and Scandinavia. The local dialect is peppered with words derived from these origins. The Dutch influence gave rise to the following, "loon" meaning a boy, "dubs" meaning mud and "crannie" which means little finger. The Nordic word for headland is "Ness" and is commonly used in place names for the area. Phrases of Gaelic origin are still in use today. These include "partan" which is the Gaelic word for crab and "connach": to spoil.

The Celts dominated the area from the 8th to the 12th centuries AD and Nigg was a district in the ancient Celtic Province of the Mearns. The rocky crags and coves became a safe haven for fishermen and several small communities sprouted up along the coast. There were regular infusions of new blood throughout the Bronze and Iron Ages, each bringing new skills to the communities in Cove, Burnbanks and Torry Village.

Tullos derived its name from a corruption of the Gaelic 'Tulach' meaning a hill. Nigg is a derivation from neuk or notch meaning peninsula. Balnagask means the village in the hollow in Gaelic. The hollow here was the one between the hill where Torry Academy now stands, and the Golf Course. The village would have been around the Motte Hill, still there in the grounds of Provost Hogg Court. It was widely believed by locals that this was an ancient burial mound but nowadays archaeologists offer an alternative theory. They now deem it to be an artificial hill fortified by a 12th century Celtic baron called Cormac de Nug (Nigg). From this vantage point the Celts could spot any approaching enemy easily.

The Celts loose tribal structure was eventually replaced by a more formal feudal system. Norman nobles were enticed northwards by marriage and the offer of land and they gradually introduced a system of hierarchical dominance. Large tracts of land were bequeathed in exchange for military and service responsibilities.

Before the 19th century, Torry was just one of many small fishing communities lying south of the River Dee. The village name was almost certainly derived from the Gaelic word TORR, meaning rounded hill or mound. The community nestled at the foot of Torry hill, close to the harbour entrance, in the area now known as Old Torry.

In 1495, the community was no more than a handful of fishermen's cottages when it gained a substantial boost. On the 11th of December King James IV granted a Royal Charter creating the town of Torry. The King was a great admirer of the town's Patron Saint and it is thought this may have been the reason for bestowing the honour. Being a free Burgh of Barony brought the inhabitants many privileges and benefits. It granted them the right to buy and sell goods, a considerable advantage in those days of restricted trade. They were allowed to appoint burgesses, elect baillies and hold weekly markets. They were also allowed to hold an annual fair on the 30th August, St. Fittick's Day. From what records survive it seems the people of Torry took very little advantage of the benefits bestowed on them.

So the people of Torry didn't get their baillies, but they could boast a Provost of Aberdeen amongst their ranks. John Collysone was elected to the post in September 1594. The council built a house for Collysone and his family at the ratepayers expense so he could stay in the city during his year in office.

Torry was the principal settlement in the Parish of Nigg. King William the Lion had granted the land to the Abbey of Arbroath. His charter is undated, but it would have been issued between 1189 and 1194. As well as the land, the Abbots also owned the ferry across the Dee and benefited greatly from its income. After the reformation in 1560 the Menzies family of Pitfodels acquired the whole of the Nigg lands.

The new landlords declined to live in Nigg and continued to live in Aberdeen. The Menzies family lived in an imposing timber-built residence on the south side of the Castlegate. The building was destroyed by fire around 1529 and was replaced by the first stone-built house in the burgh. They were an immensely powerful family, who were eminent in local politics and dominated the provostship for over 150 years during the 15th and 16th century. They remained the sole owners until the Town Council of Aberdeen bought part of the land in 1704.

There followed a period of joint ownership under the runrig system. The name is taken from the farming term 'rig and rig', meaning each ridge of the field or land belonged to different landowners. The land was cultivated in narrow strips of land or rigs. Centuries of farming this system made the crown of the rig much higher than the edges so the best soil was concentrated on top. This primitive method meant that only about a third of the seeds came to fruition. This gave rise to the old adage of

"Ane tae saw, ane tae gnaw and ane to pay the laird withaw".

When the runrig system of farming was abolished in 1785 the owners divided the land up into two halves. After arbitration the dividing line was set along the 'Manno' field or middle field. Mansefield Road is derived from Manno-field. The council obtained the land east of Mansfield Road to the Bay of Nigg and the Menzies family retained the rest. This consolidation enabled the land to be laid out in efficient farm units. The fields were enclosed by stone dykes and improved by draining and liming. Eventually the council sold off their land in nine separate plots creating several large estates such as Balnagask and Tullos.

The Old Statistical Account of 1791 describes how 652 acres were continuously cropped with oats and barley. Turnips, red and white clover, potatoes and ryegrass were also listed as crops. The rest of the land was divided between pasture, moorland and moss. A map dated around the same time shows that there were two distinct communities – Upper and Lower Torry.

Geographically the village remained isolated from its large neighbour because of the River Dee. This isolation could sometimes be an advantage as Torry was bypassed on several occasions. The Roman navy anchored in the Bay of Nigg but ignored the village before fording the Dee at Peterculter. In the Viking raid of 1153, the Norwegian Eysteinn entered the harbour with his fleet. The ruthless Viking saw little need to loot the small fishing village but set his sights on the rich pickings offered by the city of 'Apardion'. Ignoring Torry, they stormed the north shore and advanced towards Aberdeen leaving a trail of devastation in their wake.

During the War of Independence the inhabitants of Torry witnessed the burning of the city by English troops when Wallace counter-attacked. Later in the 17th century, the people of Torry witnessed the destruction of Aberdeen by Montrose and his "wild Irishes". After the battle of Alford in 1645, Montrose led the King's troops against the Covenanters of Aberdeen and left his Irish mercenaries to plunder and ransack the city. William Milne, a local farmer was killed during the battle and is buried in St. Fittick's churchyard.

Torry's isolation did not save it from the great plague. Torry, like any other medieval town or village would have been easily susceptible to any passing disease or plague. Although each house would have its own refuse heap or midden it was emptied infrequently. Poor sanitation methods meant excess rubbish, swill and excrement were frequently thrown into the narrow streets, much to the dismay of any unsuspecting passer-by. Rats and vermin roamed the streets freely so it's hardly surprising that the area was frequently visited by plague or pestilence.

The 'Black Death' arrived in the North East of Scotland in 1350. Early symptoms included a temperature, headache and nausea. Later the disease would cause fever, vomiting and a painful swelling in the lymph nodes of the groin. Death would normally occur after four days. The 'Black Death' was named after the last symptom to appear, the patient would turn purple due to respiratory failure.

The Plague was first recorded in the area in 1401 and descended on the area several times over the next two centuries. A particularly virulent strain of the plague occurred in 1647. Aberdeen's Provost closed off all entrances into the city in an effort to halt the spread of the disease. Those outside the city boundaries were left to fend for themselves. The ferry across the Dee was suspended and sentries were positioned at all entrances to the burgh to inspect travellers. Those appearing ill were prevented from entering and victims were herded into makeshift camps situated on the beach links for 'quarantine purposes'. In reality the poor unfortunates were left there to die. It's recorded that 140 inhabitants of Torry and Footdee fell victim to the disease. Despite its precautions Aberdeen faired little better as nearly 20% of the population perished.

In the 13th century Aberdeen's main export was pickled salmon. The city was trading with merchants as far away as England, Holland and the Baltic Countries. The Dee and Don fishing's supplied about 1500 barrels of salmon a year, each barrel containing about 250 lbs. of fish. Although most of the salmon was exported, there was a provision that ensured a local supplier would receive a supply if required. In the Burgh Accounts of 1581 it stated that the exporters had to supply local merchants at a set rate of threepence a pound. We also learn from this extract that a sizeable amount of the salmon was supplied from Torry: -

   "tem payt to the boy of the boitt to bring the barrell to the boitt frae Torrie schoir."

9

Later records show that the Torry small line fishermen successfully participated in the exportation of salt fish, using the cod and ling prevalent in the area. As trade expanded larger ships made the journey to Aberdeen. A large sandbank made it impossible for the bigger ships to negotiate the narrow channel. This would prove highly beneficial to Torry, as the ships would lie at anchor in the deep water at the harbour entrance. Thomas Tucker, a Cromwellian official noted the strategic importance of Torry in his report of 1656. Commenting on the harbour it states: -

> *"At the end of which foremost neck of land there is a little village called 'Footie' and at the other headland another Torye, and both nigh in harbour'mouth, and lyeing very neer unto the place where the ships usually ride…. have given opportunity of much fraude, in landing goods privately, but prevented of late by appointing the wayters by turnes, to watch those places narrowly. The trade of this place is… inwards from Norway, Eastland, Holland and France: and outwards with the salmon and pladding, commodityes caught and made hereabout in a greater plenty then any other place over the nation whatsoever".*

The people of Torry had continual trading problems with their big neighbour across the Dee. In 1675, a restraining order was placed on the inhabitants of Torry to prevent them from encroaching on Aberdeen's fishing area. Then eighteen years later the council took a similar stance to prevent the white fishers from leaving Torry to trade in Newburgh or elsewhere.

The inhabitants of Torry often had to exploit natural resources to make a living. Seaweeds were collected, dried and then burned. This resulted in kelp, an ash like substance that made an excellent fertiliser. At the end of the 18th century it was estimated that around 40 people were employed in kelp burning. Roughly 11 tons were produced in a year and that would have netted a total of £220 per annum. Kelping became unviable after the

Napoleonic Wars in 1815 because imported barytes from Spain undercut the price. Salt was another natural resource. Large cauldrons of seawater were boiled to extract the salt. However the bay area was often short of fuel so evaporation in shallow beds known as 'pans' was more common. Dulse, shellfish and peat were also taken to Aberdeen for sale.

Until the 16th century, travellers to Aberdeen from the south had to wade across the Dee at Ruthrieston, as there was no bridge. Others, preferring to keep their feet dry, would detour via Torry and travel across by ferryboat. It wasn't until the Bridge of Dee was built that a direct route to Aberdeen was possible. Once this was built Torry was more or less ignored as a main route into the city.

It wasn't until Aberdeen became a major fishing port in the late 17th and early 18th century that links with Torry started to improve. The villages dotted around the south side of the river were actually in Kincardineshire and were outside of Aberdeen's jurisdiction. It's therefore quite likely that the original inhabitants of Torry came from small hamlets scattered around the coast such as Cove or Stonehaven.

Sinclair's Statistical Account of Scotland dated 1773 lists a breakdown of professions in Torry. The account reveals that fishing was the main occupation. 36 men were manning 6 white fishing boats while there was an assortment of smaller craft crewed by older men and young boys. In addition Torry was also home to 4 blacksmiths, 2 shoemakers, a miller and a cartwright.

During the early part of the 19th century Torry would have been little more than a collection of fisherman's cottages nestling at the mouth of the Dee. Lines were stretched across the narrow space between the cottages and used to support lines, buoys, bladders and fish. In 1875 Torry consisted of just 25 houses with a population of 140.

The homes were mostly of the fisher house type. Each abode had a courtyard containing a walled midden, or waste disposal area, away from the living quarters. Each dwelling would have a thatched roof that would have to be battened down frequently because of the strong winds blowing in from

Torry around 1850 © Aberdeen Library and Information Services

the sea. This would be done with the aid of wooden spars or oars.

Each home was divided in two, the larger half was used as a kitchen and living quarters while the other was utilised as a store. The living area would be very austere indeed with just a few pieces of furniture spaced around the walls. The dirty, uneven floor was uncomfortable to walk on and the walls were blackened by soot from the fire. Smoke from the fire escaped through a small hole in the roof. Light entered the house through small holes in the wall. Wooden shutters would cover these in inclement weather or at night.

There is also pictorial evidence of 'stacked' cottages made of stone and decked with timber galleries known as 'forestaires'. These dwellings had living quarters above a shop or work premises and wooden stairs on the outside provided access. The development came slowly at first; the first modern homes were built on land reclaimed from the estuary. The first roads to be given names were Fore Close and Back Close in 1838.

Water was supplied from several wells dotted around the area. Old Torry derived its supply from Duthie's Well which stood somewhere in the vicinity of the Torry Bar. Another well in Sinclair Road was later utilised by William Fiddes & Son for manufacturing purposes.

The Aberdeen Railway Act was passed in 1845. Originally the route was going to run across Trinity Quay to a terminus at the New Market utilizing a railway bridge at Torry. However this idea was quickly rejected in favour of a route along the Vale of Tullos. This route avoided any built up area so there was very little opposition to the desecration of the valley. The simple fact was most people viewed the arrival of the Caledonian Railway as highly beneficial to the area.

The man chosen to be the rail contractor for the Nigg Parish section was James Shanks, who had run his own slate business for many years. Jimmy Shanks was a large man whose honesty and straightforward manner endeared him to workers and management alike. Sadly he died a few weeks before the project was completed.

Engineers began to plan the route and a number of problems had to be overcome. In the Vale of Tullos an embankment was built to avoid the marshy ground in the hollow. Progress through Torry went relatively smoothly but the project was beset by many problems elsewhere. A viaduct was originally planned to span an area of land south of Cove but this was abandoned in favour of a cutting. This delayed completion of the project for a year. Other difficulties included severe under-funding, general lawlessness amongst the navvies and a fatal disaster in 1846. While building the viaduct at Ferryhill, several arches collapsed killing seven men and seriously injuring another four. The Railway officially opened on Saturday 30th March 1850.

There were a couple of sites of interest to the railway enthusiast in Torry. The Craiginches signal box was located between the railway viaduct and a small marshalling yard in Girdleness Road. The box was built rather taller than normal because it was situated alongside a road bridge that would obstruct the signalman's view of his layout. These early boxes were architecturally uninspiring, a simple but perfectly adequate window arrangement was provided above a very plain brick base. Craiginches North closed because of signal network restructuring on 18th October 1981 and was demolished soon after.

The marshalling yard was used mainly to control overspill from the junction at Ferryhill. There were several rail sidings built to service local

Torry Brickworks Chimmey.
© Aberdeen Library and Information Services

industry. An ordnance map from 1900 shows a pair of sidings leading to the Craiginches Sawmill and Harper's Iron Works. The one leading to Harper's premises seemed to stretch across Wellington Road. Another siding was added later to accommodate the Blue Circle Cement Works in Kirkhill Road. None of these sidings survived into the 21st century - apart from the one leading to the cement factory, which nowadays looks neglected and overgrown.

Brick making became a successful business and in the 19th century various brickworks sprang up in and around Torry. The Torry Brickworks Company operated between 1849 and 1876. Mr John Hector, the manager of the Torry Brickworks, then helped to form another company. The Northern Patent Brick and Tile Works were established in 1867 and moved to Torry in 1883. The company leased land in Sinclair Road from the City of Aberdeen Land Association. In addition to brick making the area's supply of clay would also be used to manufacture pipes for farm drainage purposes. The company traded until 1890 when the clay at Torry was exhausted. They then moved to Strathbathie, near the Black Dog and became the Seaton Brick and Tile Company. Although the company still retained a small presence in Torry after the move.

Aberdeen was well known in the past for its export of granite to all parts of the world. It was for this reason it earned the nickname 'The Granite City'. Torry too had sizable quantities of granite and chose to exploit this resource. In earlier days oval-shaped pebbles were gathered from the shore and used as cobblestones in Aberdeen and many were exported south.

The demand for granite in the area increased following a large fire in 1741. The inferno destroyed many wooden buildings in Aberdeen and they were replaced by stone structures. During the 18th century several granite quarries were operating out of the village. Records show that John May, whose main quarry was located at Dancing Cairns, also operated from Greyhope in Torry for a time. A firm called Adam Brothers owned two quarries at Greyhope and the Bay of Nigg. They exploited the rich seams of granite and gneiss available in the area. Gneiss is a rock with similar qualities to granite and large quantities were found near Girdleness, in fact the Lighthouse was built using the compound.

The Adam Brothers were successful throughout the 18th century and brought employment to a large amount of quarrymen. At its height the industry was responsible for employing around 700 men. 'Cassies' were stones and rock produced in blocks 12" in length, 6" wide and 9" deep and the two quarries produced an inordinate amount of them. The company shipped their product to London and the south coast towns. The paving stones and 'Cassies' used on the north bank of the River Thames were from the quarries at Greyhope. It's estimated that approximately 3000 tons were exported south during the period the quarries were in existence.

Unfortunately this period of success was relatively short-lived and granite production fell quickly. The granite trade had proved to be as transient as earlier ventures. Thankfully another endeavour was around to offset the economic effects of the decline in granite manufacturing. The fishing industry was about to undergo a revolution brought on by advancements in technology and new techniques. This progress would have an enormous impact on the little village of Torry.

Old Torry Village © Aberdeen Library and Information Services

2
Fishing

From early history the inhabitants of Torry had depended mainly on fishing for their livelihood. Before the arrival of trawl fishing in the 19th century this had been done from a fleet of yawls sailing the inshore grounds. Fish were caught by means of small lines shot over the stern of the boat.

Line fishing was the principal method used by all fishermen and was practised according to the seasons. The "great line" fishing took the boats as far a forty miles offshore necessitating a few uncomfortable nights at sea in all weathers. The "small line" fishing usually allowed the men to return the same day.

The small line had 720 hooks at the regular spacing of a yard; this was used mainly during January and May when haddock was caught close inshore. During March and April their targets were cod, ling and turbot. This required the fishermen to go further offshore so great lines were used.

The great lines were similar to the small ones and varied only slightly. The deeper water required a heavier line. The main line consisted of a string, a thick piece of brown backed cord approximately sixty fathoms long. Attached to the string were snoods - short pieces of thin cord spaced at intervals of between thirty six to forty five inches along the line. Hooks were attached to the snoods by strong thread; each line could take up to 5000 hooks. The snood was bent onto the line with a knot called a clove hitch with sufficient length left to turn it back around forming a kind of lace. This prevented ravelling and twisting and was called a pen.

The head of the line went over the side first, shot across the tide so that the snoods would drift away from the main line and was anchored to the seabed by a plain, unhooked line called a tow. This was held in place by a heavy stone and a buoy marked the position of the tow on the surface. The boat was allowed to drift for a time before hauling in the line to be stowed in a wicker basket.

The herring fishing season started in mid July and lasted for six to eight weeks. The bait for the lines was perpetually in short supply and often was supplied from places as far afield as Montrose. While herring were gutted and packed wet into barrels for shipment to the markets, bigger fish had to be treated differently. Fish, such as cod, haddock and ling, were often salted or dried for winter consumption. The fish were gutted and cleaned in seawater. Then they were laid out flat in a large vat, skin side up, between layers of salt. After a number of days the fish were removed from the vat, washed again and laid out in the open air to dry. This traditional method usually took place between mid June and September.

Most people thought that sun-dried fish tasted better than those dried in kilns. However kiln drying had several advantages over the traditional method. Although a kiln was expensive for a firm to operate, the process was much quicker and the task could be completed in 48 hours rather than two weeks. Kiln drying was unaffected by seasonal weather and could also be done 24 hours a day, therefore this technique was more economically viable.

Despite these advantages, several companies persisted with the traditional method well into the 20th century. Williamson & Co. was a Shetland company who established an Aberdeen base in 1904. The main Aberdeen premises was at North Esplanade East but the company carried out the sun drying of salt fish at Girdleness, on what is now Balnagask golf course. Most of the company's output was exported to Spain, Portugal, Africa and South America. Williamson & Co. remained a family-run business until it was sold to the Claben group in 1958.

Fishing was not an easy or idyllic way of life. The boats were undecked and offered no shelter from the elements. Their clothing consisted of canvas trousers and an overcoat that offered some protection against the vagaries of the North East weather. The meals were provided in a rolled up cloth and might have consisted of roasted haddock, barley meal bannocks or a flagon of kale.

The boats varied from twenty to thirty feet in length. Each boat had a crew of six men; four to pull the oars, one to set the lines and one to land the catch. On breezy days they were able to use a mast and sail, thereby freeing the oarsmen to assist in the onboard work.

Life at sea could be dangerous and frequently fatal. One of the earliest wrecks on record has an element of poetic justice to it. Ralph the Rover was a local villain who stole the warning bell from a rocky outcrop near Girdleness. Later his ship was washed up on the same crag and he was drowned.

There have been several marine disasters around the Balnagask Headland over the years. The 'Thomas' sank in the Bay of Nigg in 1803. Thirteen years later a ship called 'Providence' came to grief at the same point. There was another shipwreck that same year when the 'Thames' ran aground on the Greyhope Rocks. Each of these tragedies resulted in many fatalities.

Probably the most famous shipwreck that happened in Torry's history occurred on the 1st April 1813. The whaler 'Oscar' was one of a group of five ships about to undertake a voyage to Greenland. The ships were already anchored in Greyhope Bay when a sudden and violent snowstorm occurred.

There was a strong westerly breeze gusting which suddenly changed direction to blow southeastwardly and the ships were buffeted by the wind. A decision to move away from the bay into deeper waters was taken and the other ships sailed out to sea. However the Oscar had delayed its departure to allow some 'wayward' crewmembers to clamber aboard. Most of the crew had been drinking but it's impossible to quantify how much this contributed to subsequent events.

The Oscar was accompanied on its journey out of the harbour by another ship, The St. Andrew. Unfortunately the wind died down soon after both vessels weighed anchor. This, combined with a heavy rolling sea and strong flood tide, made it difficult to clear Greyhope bay. Then just as quickly as it died down the storm blew up again. The ships began to drift in a north easterly direction taking them perilously close to a rocky outcrop called the Bruntscallie. The St Andrew just managed to clear Girdleness but the Oscar was not so lucky. The ship dragged her anchor and began to break up on the jagged rocks between Girdleness and the South Breakwater.

By this time a large amount off people had gathered on the shore to try and help but there was little they could do. The crew were agonizingly close to the shore but the foam and surf prevented anyone from getting to them. Members of the crew clung desperately to the rigging but were gradually washed away by the strong surf. Some of the crew felled the main mast in an effort to make a rudimentary bridge to the shore. However instead of falling towards the shore like they hoped, it collapsed in the opposite direction.

Five members of the crew, including Captain John Innes, were seen clinging vainly to the ships bow. The captain was heard shouting instructions to the people onshore but whatever he said was lost to the noise of the wind and crashing waves. The people on the shoreline watched helplessly as Captain Innes and the remainder of his crew were washed away

Miraculously there were survivors - John Jameson, the first mate and harpooner and James Venus, a crewman from South Shields. They were the only survivors out of a crew of 44. The bodies recovered from the sea were laid in one long grave at the east end of St. Fittick's Churchyard. This serves as a chilling reminder that the sea can be a great benefactor but also a cruel taskmaster.

It was a hard life at sea but the women did not have it easy either. The fishermen relied heavily on their wives and daughters to mend and bait the lines. The women's day would start as early as four in the morning when they would collect sufficient mussels for bait. Getting the mussels and baiting the hooks could take up to 9 hours per day.

More often than not the wife would accompany her husband to the water's edge and carry him on her back out to the boat so he would remain dry for the fishing. On his return she would help to gut and pack the fish and then carry the catch to Aberdeen Market in a heavy creel. Inside the creel was a smaller basket, used if she had a large load. In addition she also had to tend to their household duties.

Fisherman would normally marry young women from a similar background. If they were brought up in a fishing village they were accustomed to the heavy work and hard way of life. During the herring season Torry's single women would follow the fleet to places like Ullapool, Wick, Stornoway or Great Yarmouth. They would be employed to gut the herring or to pack the catch in barrels for export. The work was hard and the hours were long but Torry's women gained a reputation for hard work and characteristic good humour.

The Torry fishwife was a long tradition that lasted through to the early part of the 20th century. One of the last Torry fishwives was Christina Lovie Burnett who retired in 1935. Christina, usually known as 'Chirsten', sold fresh fish, bought from the market every morning. Mrs Burnett caught the train to outlying parts of Aberdeen where she would sell her goods. In addition to plying her trade around Aberdeen she also dried and salted fish.

Salmon fishing had always been one of Aberdeen's long-established industries and provided one of its main exports in the early years of the city's history. There are records of salmon fishing on the river, dating back to the 14th century. This traditional enterprise was to last right up to the 1980s.

A familiar site on a summers' day was of the salmon fishermen working on the river near the Victoria Bridge, fishing in the centuries old way with coble and sweep-net. One end of the net remained ashore while the vessel did a U-turn on the water, bringing the other end of the net to the shore. The two ends were then gathered and the net drawn in.

The fishing grounds for Torry inshore line fishers were split into distinct sections. The area from Girdleness to Gregness is called the Qheelums. Adjacent to the Qheelums is the area of sand and silt known as the Waste Bank while the area beyond that is recognized as The Grund O' Craig. The area south of the Qheelums from Gregness to Cove is identified as the Clayers.

Prior to 1776 Aberdeen had never owned more than 7 fishing boats. By the year 1778 the amount had risen to 12. Four operated out of Footdee, four fished out of Cove and the remainder berthed at Torry. The council were keen to encourage the fishing industry and provided financial assistance to fishermen to trawl for flat fish.

The number of Torry people directly employed in the fishing industry grew

Christina Lovie Burnett.
© Aberdeen Library and Information Services

rapidly. In 1790, 36 Torry men fished the North Sea in six great boats. By 1858 the Torry fishing fleet consisted of 20 boats and employed 80 men from the village. In the 1870s it was estimated there were over 160 line fishermen in the village. Each yawl had a crew of 4 or 5 men and fished 15-20 miles off the coast, south east of Girdleness. The men who crewed these yawls consisted mainly of members of the same family. Generation after generation the young men of Torry were expected to join their fathers, brothers and uncles at sea.

In isolated communities intermarrying between families was inevitable. In Torry, surnames such as Burnett, Leiper, Christie, Main, Bruce and Wood were commonplace. With such duplication of both first names and surnames it was necessary for individuals to be known by another identity. These by-names, or nicknames, were even listed in the County and Burgh Valuation Rolls. Typical examples of these by-names, also known as tee-names, taken from official records include 'Murda' 'Potchack' "Weelie's Mary' 'Lairdie' and 'Popenny'.

In 1855, the number of boats recorded in Aberdeen and Torry had risen to 43. These were mainly small boats carrying on the long tradition of line fishing. They fished mainly for haddock and cod, or herring when it was available. The traditional methods of fishing had lasted for centuries but in the later half of the 19th century the line fishermen's livelihood was about to be overtaken by a maritime revolution.

The first trawlers began fishing from the port in the 1870s. These were mainly sailing boats but trawling from such a vessel was a frustrating endeavour. John Freeland of Torry made a brief, unsuccessful attempt in 1872 but gave up soon after.

The first steam vessel to operate out of Aberdeen was a wooden tugboat called 'The Toiler'. She made her first trip out of Aberdeen on 23rd March 1882 and netted a catch of three boxes of haddock. They were sold to Thomas Davidson for £1 17s. The Toiler was fitted with a beam trawl and fished the waters from Collieston to Muchalls. The beam trawl was dragged along the seabed but was very easily damaged so the otter trawl method had been widely adopted by 1894.

The otter trawl is a mobile fish trap designed to herd fish into the net. The fish drop back into the codend where only the smallest fish can escape through the mesh. The trawl is kept open vertically by the headrope to which lots of floats are attached, and horizontally by otter boards, hence otter trawl. The otter boards are set at a particular angle to minimised drag and optimise the spread of the net. The Toiler, unable to withstand the rough North Sea conditions, was sold after a year and bigger and more efficient iron-built vessels soon followed.

The traditional fishermen were strongly opposed to trawling, as they believed it would deplete stocks in the fishing grounds. In 1883 a commission was set up to consider the complaints. The line fishermen, together with the herring fishermen of Footdee, felt trawling posed a great threat to their livelihood. They lobbied Parliament and the Fishery Board but all their efforts failed and the commission found against them. The number of steam vessels grew rapidly bringing economic prosperity to Torry and Aberdeen. By the 1890s steam trawling had virtually taken over completely. The rapid onset of this method resulted in the swift demise of the line fisherman and his yawl.

The change from sail to steam required much larger capital. The finance required was well beyond the means of most ordinary fishermen. This provided an opportunity for larger firms that owned a fleet of vessels to fill the gap. Run as a joint venture between the boat owners and the fishermen, the crew were paid no wages but received a share of the profits. The owners supplied and maintained the boats while the share fishermen supplied the nets, hooks, buoys etc.

Torry fishermen eventually adapted to the new steam trawl technology. From the traditional inshore fishing grounds they progressed further afield. They pioneered deep line fishing in the distant water grounds of Iceland, Greenland and the Faroe Islands. They also targeted larger fish in the deep water at Rockall and other Atlantic banks. Halibut, cod, ling and skate would fetch a high price at the fish market.

The Herring Fleet in Aberdeen Harbour
© *Aberdeen Library and Information Services*

For an average trip lasting 20 to 30 days, each boat would normally carry 36 baskets of great lines. Sufficient stocks of coal, ice and food would also be brought. Bait would be frozen in salt and packed in ice and stored in the fish room. The bait was normally herring but squid and mackerel were occasionally used. If they were unable to obtain bait locally they would have to sail to another port to get sufficient supplies Frequently they had to sail as far away as Stornoway to obtain the requisite amount of bait required for the trip.

Once at sea the ship would steam nearly 1000 miles to the fishing grounds on the west coast of Iceland. The journey would take around 4 days. Once in position the men would work continuously around the clock, snatching a few hours rest between shifts.

Steam Drifters were usually crewed by nine men. Compared to other fishing methods an average trip was short, usually lasting only one or two nights. The number of drifters declined greatly during the 1930s. The reasons cited for the decline were a reduced demand for herring and increased operating costs. Quite simply the shared profits were not enough to live on when split between the crewmembers

Following concerns that trawling was depleting fish stocks it soon became apparent that the levels would need to be monitored. In 1898 the Fishery Board of Scotland founded a laboratory at the Bay of Nigg. A year later a hatchery was added to the site to study the effects of releasing young plaice on fish stocks. This lasted until 1905 when it was dismantled to make way for the extension of Greyhope Road.

After the First World War a greater emphasis on fishery problems was needed so staff numbers were increased. In 1923, the Nigg Bay establishment was closed and moved to a newly purchased building in Wood Street. This building had previously been built in 1917 by the Admiralty as a hostel for apprentices at Duthie's Shipyard. However no record exists that the hostel was ever used for that purpose.

The Torry Research station joined the Marine Laboratory in 1929. Its brief was to work in the handling and preservation of fish as a food. Both these organisations excelled in operating applied research and development programmes within the fishing industry.

At the outbreak of the Second World War the Admiralty occupied the Wood Street building once more. This time the building was utilized for the training of naval personnel in wireless telegraphy. During World War II, the harbour was an important naval base; air attacks caused considerable damage and the requirements of the war effort affected trade and development. Following the war, deep-water berths were constructed at Atlantic and Pacific Wharfs.

The Marine Laboratory was re-established immediately after the war when Dr D. S. Clark became the director. Clark was famously associated with Shackleton's Antarctic expedition in 1914. There followed a period of expansion when the building was constantly extended between 1955 and 1982. A store, net loft and boiler house were built to the rear of the building. In 1969 a new building was constructed near the eastern part of Wood Street.

It housed an aquarium and large circular tank fitted with a revolving gantry to further the studies into fish behaviour.

Outside the main complex, The Marine Laboratory also occupied the old Walker Steamship Company building in Baxter Street for several years and the small fishery research ship 'Kathleen' occupied a berth in Torry Dock. The laboratory has always been subject to the requirements of economics, legislation and political whims and has expanded / contracted to suit. The last major development was completed in 1973, when a five-storey office block was built.

Throughout the 20th century Torry's prosperity remained inherently linked to events at sea. Everyone in the district either worked, or knew someone whose job depended on the maritime industry. So when a disaster happened its ramifications were felt on a community level as well as a personal one.

One such tragedy happened on Christmas Day 1935. The 'George Stroud' had sailed from Granton with its load of coal. On board was a "scratch crew" of five. Its journey had been uneventful until it sailed into the channel at Aberdeen Harbour. The weather was bad and the swell had pushed the boat off course. The trawler was adjacent to the foghorn when its hull was holed.

Frantic efforts were made to rescue the crew. A line was fired from the shore and the cook managed to grab it. Unfortunately when a wave hit the boat, he lost his grip and was washed overboard. Skipper James Phillips, Mate A. Walker and Tom Barras the Chief Engineer, who all stayed in Victoria Road, also perished in the catastrophe. George Paterson, the 2nd Engineer, was the only survivor.

Other 20th century shipwrecks included the SS 'G Koch' which was wrecked by 40-foot waves at Girdleness on 12th January 1913. Twelve crew were rescued but sadly seven men died. Evidence of this incident can still be seen to this day. At low tide, the ship's boiler can still be seen on the rocks north of the Lighthouse

The number of lives lost at sea would undoubtedly be much higher had it not been for a dedicated group of volunteers. The Aberdeen Lifeboat Station was one of the earliest in Scotland, having been established in 1802. The harbour commissioners added a second station in 1875 and by 1925 the Aberdeen lifeboat had achieved the magnificent record of 589 lives rescued. At the beginning of 1925, at the request of the harbour commissioners, the RNLI assumed control of the lifeboats and of the rocket life-saving apparatus at Torry and the North Pier. The commissioners agreed to contribute £500 a year towards their upkeep.

The Torry Rocket Brigade was instrumental in the successful

Torry Dock © Aberdeen Journals

conclusion to several rescue missions. In 1933, they helped save the lives of the crew of the 'Ben Screel' when it foundered on the rocks off Nigg Bay. However by the early 1960s, technological advancements and the introduction of radar had considerably reduced the number of incidents at sea and Aberdeen No 2 station and the Torry life saving apparatus were closed on the 30th June 1962.

The fishing industry in Aberdeen had expanded well beyond its humble origins. It had grown from a few fishermen making a living at the mouth of a shallow estuary to a multi-million-pound industry employing thousands of people. This was due in no small part to the expansion and development of the harbour area and it's this aspect we'll concentrate on in the next chapter.

3
The Harbour

The history of fishing in Torry and Aberdeen is intrinsically linked to the harbour. Around 2,000 BC, immigrants from the Rhineland and Holland used the River Dee estuary occasionally as a base for fishing. The Romans are also reported to have used the harbour to supply soldiers in the area. However this is mere speculation, as the first recorded mention of the harbour didn't happen until the 12th century. In AD 1136, King David 1st of Scotland granted the Bishops of Aberdeen the right to tax a tenth of the profits made by all ships trading at the port.

Improvements were made to the port when trade links with Scandinavia and the Baltic were established after the middle ages. In 1582 the first crane to load and unload ships was used. 14 years later King James VI granted a charter to raise funds for improvements.

In 1607, a bulwark was planned along the south of the estuary so that when the tide went in and out it would scour the harbour and make it deeper. However there were several delays and work didn't begin for another five years. The master mason put in charge of the project was James McKeane. The building of the bulwark became a labour of love for the Torry people. Jasper Milne the piper and Andrew Inglis the drummer serenaded the workforce while they grafted.

The bulwark was built from uncemented stone and large oak beams. The pier was extended by ten feet in 1649 at a cost of £18 6s 8d. Occasionally because of the ravages of weather it was deemed necessary to repair it. In 1707 the timber from a Dutch boat wrecked at the Black Dog was used to renew it. The bulwark lasted until 1810 when it was demolished on the recommendation of the harbour engineers. They took this action because the structure was thought to be responsible for causing tidal disturbances along the harbour basin.

Up until the early 17th century, a huge rock partly blocked the harbour mouth. The large stone was known as "Knock Maitland" or Craig Matellan".

Torry Harbour © Aberdeen Library and Information Services

The authorities had tried for many years to get rid of it as it posed a serious hazard to shipping. Even explosives hadn't managed to break it up into moveable pieces. Then David Anderson, a local trouble-shooter from Finzheugh, stepped forward. Anderson, who already rejoiced in the nickname "Davie do a'thing" or "Davie Doo" for short, convinced the Council that he could do it and they willingly provided the materials and labour he demanded.

At low tide, Davie supervised as a squad of labourers attached empty barrels to the rock with strong ropes. As the tide came in, the barrels lifted the rock clear of the channel bed and a flotilla of small boats towed the rock into the estuary where it was dumped well clear of the shipping lanes.

27 years later, the harbour mouth silted up completely when a huge sandbar blocked the channel. "The Bar" was a large bank of silt and sand that extended across the mouth of the river. At low tide the river was only around two or three feet deep. This made it extremely difficult to navigate a safe passage through the harbour entrance. Several steps were taken to improve it to no avail as picks and shovels made no impression.

However, just as city officials had resigned themselves to the loss of the fish export trade to the continent, the Dee swept down in spate and cleared away the obstruction. Even so, there was never more than a few feet of water at the harbour bar and the prevailing Northeast drift of sand ensured the problem would eventually have occurred again.

Trade increased to record levels following the union of parliaments with England in 1707 but the harbour bar still limited further expansion. Extensive engineering work would have to be undertaken to improve the condition of the harbour. John Smeaton, the eminent engineer, recommended the building of the North Pier. Completed in 1780, the 1,200-foot pier increased the depth of water and provided shelter at the entrance.

Another famous engineer, Thomas Telford, later proposed the extension of the North Pier and suggested building a southern breakwater. His report recommended the adoption of a proper plan for managing the river and harbour entrance and improving the interior parts of the estuary. Luckily sufficient funds were available and Telford's suggestions were accepted.

The old south breakwater eventually extended 800 feet northwards to within 250 feet of the North Pier. It was completed in 1815 at a cost of £14,000 and became known as the 'Skate's Nose'. However Aberdeen fast became a busy seaport and further upgrades to the entrance were deemed necessary.

A 19th century act of parliament handed control of the harbour to a body of commissioners and they set about making the improvements. In 1829, the harbour board was augmented by six members elected from the guildry and incorporated trades. Trinity Quay and Regent Quay were constructed with Waterloo and Pocra quays following in quick succession.

The Raik Dyke had been constructed as an attempt to help regulate the flow of the Dee in 1831. It prevented water from the Dee flowing past Torry. However the Dyke was not a great success and caused a considerable fall in the volume of the main stream. Therefore the Victoria Dock was proposed as an alternative. Work began in 1841 and the project was completed seven years later at a cost of £122,000. For the first time Aberdeen had a stable water level within the dock area allowing ships to be unloaded by steam derrick. The new dock received royal approval when Queen Victoria and the Prince Consort berthed their yacht there in September 1848.

The need for more quay space was identified and gradually the areas of shoals and mudflats between Aberdeen and Torry disappeared to be replaced by solid structures. Provost Blaikie's Quay was built in 1834 followed by the first phase of Albert Quay in 1860. Provost Matthews' Quay and Provost Jamieson's Quay was constructed during the 1880s after the Dee was diverted. The former Raik and Stell fishing areas became the network of streets west of the Albert Basin and the Upper Dock.

While these improvements were made, the Girdleness Lighthouse was commissioned. A wave-cut platform extends right around the Girdleness Peninsula, making the water deceptively shallow to unwary seafarers. The lighthouse was built to alert ships to this danger. It was designed by Robert Stevenson and built by Aberdeen contractor James Gibb. The 37 metre high tower cost £11,000 to erect and equip. The circular whitewashed lighthouse tapers upwards to reach a corbelled gallery topped by an iron cupola. The Harbour Master of Aberdeen requested the light in 1813 after the whaling ship Oscar was wrecked near the point. He felt it was vital to prevent such a tragedy from occurring again.

The light had a new design, showing 2 distinct lights from the same tower, one above the other. Each silver-plated mirror was 21 inches in diameter. The lower light consisted of 12 lamps and reflectors arranged like a garland in a glazed gallery built round the outside of the tower at 115 feet. The lower one was highly decorated with cast-iron panels. The upper light consisted of 18 reflectors at 185 feet above sea level. The beam flashes twice every 20 seconds and is visible from 19 miles at sea in normal conditions. The Astronomer Royal, Professor George Airy, (later Sir George) visited Girdleness in 1860. He described it as the best lighthouse he had seen.

Girdleness Lighthouse, which contains 192 steps, is named after the rocky promontory it overlooks. The lamp was lit for the first time at sunset on 15th October 1833. At first the light was fixed, but a revolving light was installed

The Lighthouse by E.J. Roberts © Aberdeen Library and Information Services

in 1890. The lower lantern was discontinued at this time. Before electrification, the lamps were powered by pressure-vaporised paraffin, which burned at a rate of 9.5 gills an hour. The lamp and reflectors were activated through an arc covering the entire seafront by a clockwork motor and imbedded in a mercury bath to attain an even pressure. Curved mirrors replaced the upper light in 1948. Incidentally the original lower lamp was discovered at Inchkeith in 1986 and restored. When the lighthouse was fully automated in 1991, the three keepers' cottages were sold off as private housing.

Beside the lighthouse there are two large pylons that are part of a 14-station navigational network called the Differential Global Positioning System. The DGPS was inaugurated in 1998 and its introduction led to another familiar landmark being made redundant.

Immediately to the south of the Girdleness Lighthouse stands the foghorn, known locally as the "Torry Coo". The foghorn had blasted out its familiar warning call across Greyhope Bay for well over a century. The instrument was usually put into operation when visibility fell below 5 miles. James Dove and Co installed the last machine in 1902 under supervision from

The Torry Coo. © Gordon Bathgate

William Burness, the Lighthouse Commissioner's Engineering Inspector. Compressed air was passed into the rotating siren from cylinders every two minutes. This resulted in four blasts, two high and two low notes, which could be heard 20 miles at sea. Three 25 horsepower engines, each producing air pressure of 30lbs, were used to power the compressed air cylinders.

Even when the lighthouse was blacked out for security reasons the foghorn continued to operate ensuring mariners negotiated the tricky waters around Aberdeen safely. It was graded as a "Category A Listed Building" in 1967 before being decommissioned in the late eighties. An attempt by the Northern Lighthouse Board to have it demolished was opposed by local conservationists in 2003. Luckily the council supported the appeal and the plans for demolition were thrown out. The foghorn was given a fresh lick of paint in 2005 but no firm plans for it's future have been announced.

To assist mariners the two leading lights were built on Sinclair Road in 1842. Both lights were made of cast iron with raised lines towards the base to suggest masonry construction. A metal ladder on the side provides access to the lantern for maintenance purposes. Their sophisticated design and construction reflected the status of Aberdeen as a port. The one further west was built on an elevated site so a boat coming up the channel could see both lights. Despite today's sophisticated navigational aids this ancient method is still used to guide ships into Aberdeen Harbour - two fixed red lights or green if the channel is closed. In the olden days the keeper lived at 142 Sinclair Road beside the second lighthouse. It was his duty to maintain both of the lamps and ensure they were in good working condition. Nowadays the roundhouse on the North Pier controls the lights.

The North Pier protected the navigation channel to the north but plans were proposed to extend it. If this were to happen the South Breakwater would have to be re-sited farther east. Work on the new South Breakwater began in 1869. It was built using concrete blocks made from stones taken from the Bay of Nigg. Where the foundation ran under water great spars of Oregon pine costing £55 apiece were set in place. Wagons carrying huge sacks of liquid concrete were ferried along this makeshift platform and the concrete was poured into position.

The new South Breakwater extended to 1000 feet seawards and was completed in 1874. The light tower at the tip was added three years later. Once the new breakwater was finished the old one was partly demolished back to the low water mark. These changes regulated the flow of water better and annulled the need for constant dredging. The harbour defences were now complete and the port was on the brink of great prosperity, a prosperity in which Torry was to share.

The South Breakwater was seriously damaged during a fierce storm in the latter part of 1936. The stone structure was breached near its tip and a plan of action was swiftly put in place to rebuild it. Construction work commenced on the 5th July 1937. A massive 'Titan' crane was erected on the site to place large slabs of masonry into position. The steam-driven behemoth was frequently unable to carry out its duties due to bad weather. The project was also completely suspended during World War II. Work was eventually completed in time to shelter the harbour from the effects of the winter gales in 1954.

In 1871, Aberdeen Harbour Commissioners acquired the Raik, Stell and Midchingle salmon fishing rights, along with the sea-netting rights from Broadhill to Girdleness. This allowed them to develop the harbour without hindrance by private individuals. It cost the commissioners £30,000 to achieve that freedom. The harbour board continued to carry out commercial salmon fishing on the Dee into the 1980s.

The advent of steam trawling in the 1880s meant a significant increase of activity and further developments to accommodate the fishing industry. In the first half of the 20th century, the entrance channel was deepened; transit sheds were built and a large pontoon dock provided.

In 1960, a new port authority and board were established. This ushered in a new era of sustained growth and development. Waterloo, Regent, Trinity and Upper Quays underwent a facelift as part of a significant rebuilding programme and Victoria Dock was dredged to offer better access for bigger ships. The dock gates were removed, as were the Regent and St Clement bridges. Perhaps the most significant development was the port starting up a 24-hour operation.

The fish market was extensively reconstructed but all this development had arrived too late to help the beleaguered fishing industry. In the early 1950s there were roughly 35 great line fishing boats sailing from Torry Dock. The number steadily declined when economics forced many vessels out of business. By the mid 1960s the fleet had dwindled to the point where there were only four 'liners' left and the fishing industry went into recession. However Aberdeen had another string to its bow by this time. The city's economic saviour was looming beyond the horizon of the North Sea.

The arrival of the offshore oil and gas industries resulted in a remarkable programme that would virtually rebuild the harbour and transform it into one of the most modern ports in Europe. During the '60s, Pacific Wharf was further developed to provide additional deep-water berthing and the navigation channel was deepened. The harbour board built a new roll-on roll-off terminal and a second terminal for international ferries was later established.

By 1984, nine oil bases had been developed at the port. However as the offshore industry expanded, one traditional industry suffered a terminal decline. The lack of orders in the ship building industry caught up with the port's last remaining yard and the fine tradition of shipbuilding in Aberdeen ended with its closure in 1991.

The location was renamed as Telford Dock and redeveloped to provide a new multi-berth deep-water and ship repair facility - This was the largest single investment project at the port during the 20th century. The dock commemorates Thomas Telford, who shaped much of the modern harbour. The names of the quays - Russell's, Duthie's, Hall's and Clipper - are another link with history, recalling the age of building clipper ships.

Aberdeen Harbour handles around 25,000 vessel movements a year. The Roundhouse handles navigation control for the harbour. The Roundhouse, so called because of its shape, was first established in 1803. However it would seem that after two centuries the Roundhouse's days may be numbered. Ambitious plans for a £3million operations centre were unveiled in February 2005 and building work was undertaken shortly afterwards. The new operations centre will integrate all marine operations in one location and the new building will offer commanding views over the port's main arteries. The project is due to be completed in 2006.

The evolution of Aberdeen as a world-class port continues into the 21st century. The redevelopment of deep-water Matthews Quay provided a third roll-on/roll-off terminal, handling international traffic. Today, Aberdeen Harbour handles around 4 million tonnes of cargo annually, with some £1.5 billion, and inputs over £100 million a year into the local economy.

4
The Torry Battery

Visitors to the south side of the harbour may be forgiven for overlooking the Torry Battery. The once imposing coastal defence site has become a hollow, neglected shell. Surrounded by the Balnagask Golf Course and dwarfed by the Girdleness Lighthouse, the old ruins offer an excellent panoramic view of the harbour. Beyond are the impressive towers of the modern city, with the ancient spires of Old Aberdeen in the distance.

However what's left of the battery is less impressive. The outer walls remain virtually intact and offer shelter from the bitter cold winds sweeping in from the North Sea. Inside, only a handful of crumbling ruins remain of the fortress infrastructure. It's hard to believe that this empty husk was once home to up to 200 soldiers and officers, an infirmary, cookhouse, storeroom and gun emplacements

On a 1908 plan of the battery, a drawbridge is marked on the exterior of the gate. Fittings on the inside of the gateway may once have supported this drawbridge. The ruins of the guardhouse stand just inside the main gate. Inside is all that remains of the central fireplace in the guardroom. The fireplace and chimney are made from a mixture of granite and brick. To the left and right of the fireplace are two small rooms that are the remnants of cells used to house prisoners.

There is also a small granite building with a crow-stepped roofline at the eastern end of the battery. This was a coal store that once stood next to the officers' quarters and mess and may have been used to supply the fires in those buildings. The cookhouse still stands in the centre of the southern curtain wall of the battery. The pentagonal building was located near to a series of four barrack rooms.

A large number of slit windows still survive in the south curtain wall of the battery along with various scars. These are the remnants of buildings which once lined the inside of the battery wall. They included storerooms for coal, utensils, bedding and straw. These and other buildings had been demolished

The Torry Battery. © Gordon Bathgate

in 1959. The gap in the wall is the remains of a small exit. It would presumably have had a large gate but no trace of it now exists.

Only two of the nine gun emplacements survive. The easternmost gun emplacement is the most intact. Adjacent to the emplacement is the ammunition store used to house shells. The metal rail on which the gun swivelled is still intact and was mounted on granite blocks jointed together with metal dowels. The other one's tracks have been removed but three seats have been built into the semi-circular stanchion. It's highly likely most of the emplacements were removed, but it's possible that some may survive underground. It's thought the large grassy mound in the centre of the battery may cover one or more of the other gun emplacements.

There had been several defence structures at the harbour prior to the 18th century. A blockhouse was first built in the 1490s as a response to deter a perceived threat of an English sea-borne attack. It stood on the sandy outcrop called the Sandness, roughly where Pocra Quay stands today. During times of conflict a barrier made of iron chains and ship masts blocked the mouth of the Dee. The blockhouse was rebuilt several times and used occasionally as a place of execution for pirates. It became the primary defence for the city for many centuries but the need for a more permanent structure was identified.

A new battery soon replaced the blockhouse. This one was situated on the beach at the end of the Esplanade and stood approximately where the public toilets are now. In August 1794 it was thought an invasion by French troops lead by Napoleon I was imminent. Arthur Gibbon formed the Aberdeen Battery Company to protect the city and the harbour entrance from enemy ships. Incredibly each volunteer received three guineas bounty and the freedom of the city of Aberdeen as an incentive. For this they assembled twice weekly and received military training. The Government also provided clothing and a weekly allowance. The non-commissioned officers and privates received one shilling for each day they were on duty.

In the spring of 1797, it was thought an invasion by the Spanish was forthcoming and steps were taken to protect the northeast shoreline. The parishioners of Nigg made an offer to the Lord Lieutenant of the County "without expense to the government". The minutes of the preparations reveal that 49 Torry men and 31 men from Cove volunteered for small arm training or to man great guns. The documents also divulge that local fishermen offered the use of their boats to convey soldiers along the coast, while the farmers offered their horse and carts to transport military supplies. An inventory of crops and livestock was also taken so that they could be removed or destroyed if the Spanish came ashore. The papers disclose that in the Parish of Nigg there were 52 carts, 85 horses, 321 cows, 447 bolls of bear (a type of barley), 642 bolls of oats and meal, 19 bolls of pease, 293 bolls of potatoes, and 10,580 stones of hay at the Lord Lieutenant's disposal.

There is no evidence to suggest that any large defence structure existed on the Girdleness Headland prior to this period. Although there are earlier references to a structure called "Wallace's Castle", which is thought to have stood at the north side of the Bay of Nigg. However this was probably just a rather grandiose name for a simple watch house. In fact there were several such constructions dotted around the area. A watch house was placed at

Greyhope Bay; a sentry was positioned here to ring a warning bell at the first sign of a ship approaching. Another watch house was erected beside the Baron's Cairn and its foundations were still evident in the early part of the 20th century.

However Tullos Hill and the Balnagask Headland was certainly used for training purposes; in fact the Bay of Nigg was the scene of the last recorded pistol duel in Aberdeen. Lieutenant Booth of the 1st Regiment Aberdeen Volunteers was embroiled in the situation when his clerk, 16-year-old Robert Forsyth, was injured during an altercation with a soldier from another regiment. Forsyth's hand had been cut after the soldier, an Ensign Livingston, from the Stirlingshire Regiment, had lunged at him with a sword. When Booth heard about the incident he lodged a complaint against the visiting soldier. Livingston was outraged and challenged Lieutenant Booth to a duel. So at dawn on the 26th June 1805, Livingston and Booth met at the Bay of Nigg and drew their pistols. There followed a swift duel that left Lieutenant Booth seriously injured with a single gunshot wound. Sadly, he died 16 weeks later of his injuries.

Like other units across the country, there were strict guidelines stating where the Aberdeen Volunteers could be deployed. No unit would be allowed to travel outside a 5-mile radius of the city. Only a direct order from the king could countermand this directive, and even then only if an invasion was imminent. However the threatened invasion never came and the original fort was allowed to fall into disrepair. Protracted negotiations between the city council and the board of ordnance ended without agreement, as neither side was willing to fund repairs or meet the cost of a new battery.

It wasn't until half a decade had passed that work began on the second battery and France was again the enemy. Napoleon III adopted a belligerent policy after the Crimean War and this threat finally prompted city officials into sanctioning the building of the battery. In 1854, a representative from the Royal Engineers visited Aberdeen to help plan the construction. Lieutenant Colonel Ford, based at Fort George recommended the fort be built at Torry Point, which was at that time called Shortness. A suggestion to site the battery at the Bay of Nigg had been rejected earlier.

Work commenced on the new fort in 1857 and was designed by R. R Anderson R.E. The building was constructed in a mixture of quarried granite blocks, granite fieldstones and brick. The barracks accommodated approximately 90 men and by the time work was completed the project had cost £7,236.

The Torry Battery was eventually completed on the 24th October 1860 and operated by members of the 1st Aberdeenshire Royal Garrison Artillery (Volunteers). These men were forerunners of the Territorial Army. They were trained like the regular army, but would remain as civilians until called upon. The troops adopted a blue uniform similar in style to the one worn by the Royal Artillery, albeit with ample amounts of braiding as embellishments.

The fortress was fully equipped with weapons to prevent unauthorised ships from entering the harbour. These included nine heavy guns: six 68-pounders plus three 10-inch shell guns and were armed by placing the shell into the muzzle. Later in 1861, two of the heaviest known armaments of the day were delivered: 200lb Armstrong guns. They were described as being capable of 'dropping a ball from Torry as far as Newburgh'. Another muzzle loading rifle was added in 1880. Prior to the First World War a couple of 6-inch breech-loading rifles were added. These guns were placed on CP MK II mountings and were similar in style as the others, except that the shells were loaded from the rear. The upgrade cost £5,640 and was completed within two years.

The weapons were never fired at enemy ships but there is a record of them being used to try to help recover the body of a local businessman. Local shipyard owner Walter Hood was drowned in 1862 after slipping in the dark and falling into the harbour. The battery guns were fired in the hope that the concussion would bring the body to the surface but grappling irons were needed to recover the corpse.

The battery was partially dismantled in 1895. The guns and mountings were returned to the ordnance stores at Leith. By 1901 Aberdeen had two heavy batteries and six garrison artillery companies and all of them trained at Torry Point from time to time. On the 8th June 1905 a strip of land along Baxter Street and Victoria Road was sold to the Commissioners for the Lord High Admiral for the United Kingdom. This was to allow the road approaching the Torry Battery to be widened, giving troops easier access to Torry Point. This move was prompted by civil unrest in Russia.

The gunners may have been amateurs but they acquitted themselves well. Thirteen volunteers from the city batteries served with various military units in South Africa during the Boer War. The units proved how well trained they were when they won the Playfair Cup at the Scottish National Artillery camp in 1903 and the King's Cup the following year. The Volunteer Force was re-organised following Lord Haldane's reforms in 1908 and became known as the Territorial Force, later the Territorial Army. The units were restructured to become the 1st and 2nd City of Aberdeen Batteries, Royal Field Artillery, 2nd Highland Ammunition Column, Royal Field Artillery and the North Scottish Royal Garrison Artillery.

The battery wasn't staffed on a permanent basis until the First World War in 1914. However it was the gunners, not the Torry Point guns, which saw action during the Great War. The volunteer gunners were deployed in support of the 51st Highland Division on the Western Front at High Wood, Ypres and Arras.

The guns remained in position between the wars but the battery wasn't fully staffed again until the outbreak of World War II. During each of the wars the roads leading to the battery were blocked off and only military staff were allowed access to Torry Point. Certain civilians were allowed in the restricted area but only after both they and their families had undergone a strict security check by police officers from Lodge Walk.

Once again, the city's territorial artillery force left to serve overseas and saw action in North Africa, Sicily, France, Belgium, Holland, Italy and Germany. In their absence the battery was manned by a succession of regular army artillery formations including men from the Home Guard and the City of Liverpool Battalion of the Royal Artillery. The regular army finally

The Battery Guns. © Aberdeen Journals

vacated the battery when the war finished in 1945 and the Territorials took over once more.

The site was also used as emergency accommodation during two phases of housing shortages. The first period started in 1935 when twenty families were charged between 3/6d and 5/6d per week for their lodgings at the battery. This lasted until 1938 when the huts were declared unfit for human habitation

Aberdeen was heavily bombed during the war and this created a severe housing shortage. Many families were either homeless or living in overcrowded conditions. The buildings and Nissen Huts of the Torry Battery were once again used to alleviate the problem while the house-building programme was undertaken. This arrangement was never officially sanctioned so the families were technically squatting. Other "squatters" also targeted the old clubhouse at Balnagask Golf Course.

Across Britain people were squatting in buildings which had been evacuated by the military authorities as these often had electricity, gas and running water. Prime Minister Clement Attlee ordered that there was to be no eviction of squatters on these sites. In fact the attitude of the government seemed to be that such places were to be made habitable.

Aberdeen City Council had been prepared for this situation for quite some time. In January 1946, the council had resolved to convert Torry Battery into nine single rooms, eight two-roomed and two three-roomed houses, at a cost of £300. However the proceedings were held up by the military authorities. The council eventually took over the camps in September 1946, organising sanitary arrangements, lighting and installing a communal water supply. The rent was set at eight shillings per hut.

At the height of the housing shortage it's thought as many as 44 families were staying there. It's apparent that there that there was a great community spirit amongst the tenants. Families often congregated along what was known as Main Street, the path running between the two rows of barracks buildings on the landward side of the battery. The last tenants moved out in 1952.

The battery guns were briefly re-activated during the 1956 Suez Crisis prior to full decommissioning in 1957. The site was sold within months to the local council who have retained ownership since then. It was during this period that the remains became home to around thirty different species of migratory birds. Blackcaps and willow warblers are regular visitors in the spring while redwings fly in from their Scandinavian breeding grounds in the autumn. The ruins can also be used as an ideal vantage point to watch dolphins and porpoises swim in the harbour.

In 1964, a local entrepreneur approached the council with a plan to convert the ruins into a hotel but this was rejected. The battery was partly demolished and the site abandoned. The remaining buildings were left to crumble while the parade ground was littered by debris. At this time calls were made to demolish the eyesore but thankfully the council never completed the demolition. Instead, most of the rubbish and rubble inside the perimeter walls was cleared and the ground became a public park and picnic area in 1971. The scheme was jointly financed by the city council and the Scottish Development Department. The spiked iron fence around the fort

The Torry Battery with fish racks in front © Aberdeen Journals

was removed, the car park was laid out and the retaining walls were reinstated, complete with nesting holes for the birds.

For over forty years the vast majority of Aberdonians had ignored the ruins of this once important building but slowly that began to change. The battery was the ideal focal point to view a magnificent spectacle during the last decade of the 20th century. Thousands of people lined up alongside the ruins when Aberdeen hosted the Cutty Sark Tall Ships Race. The magnificent sailing vessels sailed past the fort twice, once in 1991 and again in 1997.

Recently another landmark was added to the Torry Point skyline. The Torry Heritage Society erected a monument to seafarers who lost their lives at sea. It took the form of a granite cairn below a stainless steel cross. A granite slab with a suitable inscription is incorporated into the base of the cairn. The Lord Provost of Aberdeen performed the unveiling on September 12th 2001. Just one month later, Historic Scotland recognised the battery as a place of historic and military importance. The site is now listed as an ancient monument and it is an offence to damage the structure in any way.

The battery played host to another prestigious event on June 3rd 2002. A crowd of over a hundred people gathered to observe the culmination of Aberdeen's diamond jubilee celebrations. One of Torry's oldest residents, 91-year-old Ted Munro, lit the 12-foot beacon to commemorate the Queen's 50-year reign.

The council have identified the fort as a resource that is sadly underused and funding has been earmarked to restore the site to prominence. A maritime centre and museum are just some of the schemes planned for the battery site. After decades of neglect, it seems there is renewed enthusiasm for this once popular destination.

5
Craiginches Prison

Craiginches Prison is situated high on the banks of the River Dee, 300 yards south of the Wellington Suspension Bridge. Its imposing grey granite walls have incarcerated thousands of prisoners since it was built in the late 19th century.

How the prison came to be built at this location is worth a brief diversion. Before Craiginches was completed, prisoners were located at Lodge Walk in Aberdeen city centre. On 20th October 1394, King Robert III sanctioned a royal charter for the building of a courthouse and tolbooth in the Castlegate. The 'Leigh Tolbooth' became the council chamber and courthouse and the 'High Tolbooth' became the city's first prison known as 'Mide O' Mar'. The Old Tolbooth Prison complete with condemned cell was erected between 1616 and 1629 and part of it remains to this day. It was opened as a museum in the 1990s but was closed a few years later due to financial cutbacks. However people can still visit it occasionally when the council opens its amenities to the public and holds what it calls a "Doors Open Day". Its revival as a museum has not been ruled out if funding becomes available in the future.

A correction house was built in 1636. This establishment was one of the first of its kind in Scotland and was the brainchild of Provost Alexander Jaffray who took office during the previous year. In the prison records it describes the inmates as: -

"All vagabonds, strong and sturdie beggares, idle and maisterless personyes, strong in bodie and habill to work, servants disobedient to maistria, children disobedient to parentis, leud leivars, pyikers, common scolds and incorrigible harlottis not amending to the discipline of broadcloths, kerseys, seys and other course cloths'. The building stood in the vicinity of Correction Wynd, to which it eventually gave its name".

In October 1809 the new Bridewell was opened at a site at the north end of Rose Street. Its name was changed to 'West Prison' in 1842. A new courthouse was erected behind the tolbooth in 1819. It had a jail extending along Lodge Walk that was known as the 'East Prison'.

Between 1819 and 1864, provision for penal establishments in Aberdeen was more than adequate with both the newer East Prison and the West Prison in existence. However on 1st March 1864 the West Prison was closed and the prisoners were transferred to the East Prison. The council purchased the land for £3,000 and demolished the old Bridewell in 1868. They used the site for their new police headquarters, which eventually opened in 1895.

The prisons were miserable and overcrowded places and city officials soon recognised the need for a brand new purpose-built facility. With space in the city centre at a premium, and little or no scope for expansion, a site on the outskirts of Aberdeen was sought.

Messrs D. Andrew and Co, Aberdeen, built Craiginches Prison at a cost of £19,000. Work commenced on 16th October 1889 and was eventually occupied on 9th June 1891. Mr Rutledge, the incumbent governor of Aberdeen Prison, agreed to postpone his retirement to supervise the transition period.

The location of the new prison in Torry caused a few difficulties. The transportation of prisoners from the police office to the prison prompted a great deal of debate at the meetings of the Watching, Lighting and Fires Committee. Eventually it was agreed that the council would purchase a horse and van for the purpose, but only after the Prison Commissioners of Scotland agreed to pay an annual sum of £75 for the conveyance of prisoners. Payments were made in quarterly instalments and the horse drawn 'Black Mariah', with its discreet window blinds, soon became a familiar sight on its route to the prison.

The prison and its associated buildings encompassed an area of 4 acres and was originally intended to house both male and female prisoners. The buildings inside the prison compound were designed using the rock-faced ashlar of the old Palace Hotel in Union Street as a template. The prison consisted of two halls, each with a chapel and a capacity for 50 prisoners. The female block and quarters for female warders were attached to 'B' Hall. The male section, 'A' Hall, was expanded a few years after the prison was opened to accommodate another 45 prisoners.

Buildings outside the prison consisted of the governor's house and a block of 4 staff quarters, all in the prison drive. The gate lodge, which housed the general office, completed the original buildings. The reception block was added around the same time as 'A' hall was enlarged. When associated labour was introduced a work shed was built in the grounds. The shed was enlarged several times between 1930 and 1961.

After the Second World War, 'B' Hall was altered. Cell walls were removed to make more room for workspace. The bottom section of the hall was partitioned off to make a small, self-contained female remand unit while the upper part of 'B' Hall was converted into an execution block

The original condemn cell and execution chamber were located at the far end of 'B' Hall. There were several cells situated beyond an archway used by the prisoners to slop out. The cells on the second floor were converted to house the execution complex. Two cells on the right hand side were altered and became the condemn cell. The three cells on the left were converted to become the execution chamber. Both rooms had double doors and, when opened, they created a corridor leading from the condemn cell straight through to the execution chamber.

The beam that supported the hangman's noose was mounted in the centre of the three cells on the top floor. The doorway was built halfway up with brick, leaving only half the normal door; this brickwork was used to support the beam. Nevertheless, despite its elaborate construction, this drop was never used. On the 1st February 1956 at Aberdeen High Court, a prisoner by the name of Robert James Boyle was sentenced to death. He was due to hanged on the 10th March 1956. Special orders were drawn up with Mr Wade and Mr Smith being appointed as executioners. However it never happened and Boyle's sentence was eventually commuted to life imprisonment. The beam and the drop platform were moved from 'B' hall to the new condemn cell / execution chamber in 1962.

In 1961, 'B' Hall was rebuilt into its original form to accommodate the increasing numbers of prisoners. A new block was added to house the small number of females held at this time. During this period major alterations were made to the prison, including a new office and store block added to the gatehouse. Also added were a visiting room, new surgery and an educational centre for handicrafts and classes. Later a new dining hall, engineer's office, work shed and execution block were planned and completed.

The execution block was only used on one occasion for the hanging of Henry John Burnett, who incidentally was the last man to hang in Scotland. Burnett was convicted of the shooting of his lover's husband Mr Thomas Guyan. The couple had met while working at J. R. Stephen's fish house in Torry.

Henry John Burnett was sentenced to death at the High Court at Aberdeen on 25th July 1963. Despite introducing considerable evidence supporting Burnett's history of mental illness during the trial, all pleas for clemency by the defence council were rejected. Burnett steadfastly refused to appeal against his sentence and returned to Craiginches to occupy the new condemn cell.

The condemn cell itself was wood panelled on each wall, with private toilet facilities for the prisoner and another for the staff. In an effort to conceal the last route the condemned prisoner would take, hidden doors were built into the wood panelling. Burnett was not a problematic prisoner and was always reasonably affable to the warders. He even identified the doors in which he would take his last walk. He pointed to the joints in the skirting boards to his escorts.

As it happened, Burnett never went through those concealed doors. It was not until the hangman and his assistant arrived to prepare for the event that a problem was discovered. They indicated that the drop platform and the hooks on the roof had been erected facing the wrong direction. In its present position, the prisoner would have to be manoeuvred around the execution chamber before he could walk onto the platform. By the time the mistake was discovered it was too late to make any alternations. Instead it was decided to take Burnett out onto the landing where the duty magistrates were waiting to witness the hanging, then into the front door to the execution chamber, straight onto the platform.

Not surprisingly, feelings were running high within the prison at the time of the hanging. Both the staff and prisoners were edgy and the warders had to use a great deal of tact and diplomacy when dealing with prisoners. On the morning of the hanging the prisoners were fed in their cells as normal. Several elaborate acts of subterfuge were made to ensure that no prisoner could identify the hangman or witness the execution. After breakfast all those located in the cells and the east side of 'A' Hall, adjacent to the Condemn Cell, were moved to the other side of the hall. After all the prisoners were accounted for, the warders were made to change galleries and then change again.

The Scottish Office supplied the rope and charged the city council £10 for it. They also submitted an alphabetic list of six names of possible executioners. The first name on the list was Harry Allen from Manchester and magistrates chose him to perform the hanging.

Henry Burnett's hanging took place at the allotted time of 8am on the 15th August 1963. This had been the first execution to take place in Aberdeen since 1857. Witnessing events were two magistrates, Baillies Williamson and Middleton, plus the prison doctor. In addition, the arresting police constable and inspector were there to officially identify the prisoner. Also present were the prison chaplain, Rev. John Dickson, the minister of St. Fittick's Church, and Canon Charles Glennie of St Peter's Episcopal Church. They were there to attend his spiritual needs but by all accounts Burnett remained calm throughout the procedure

The execution procedure is worth a brief explanation, if only to give an indication of what a grim and distressing experience it must have been to endure, both for prisoner and warder alike. Flanked by two prison officers, Burnett was escorted from the condemn cell to a platform containing a trap door. Harry Allen placed a white cotton hood over Burnett's head and positioned the noose round his neck whilst his assistant strapped his ankles. The noose was adjusted so that the eyelet was tight under the angle of the left jaw, held in place by a rubber washer. At the appointed time, the hangman removed the safety pin from the base of the operating lever and pushed it to release the trap doors. The procedure went off without a hitch and Burnett's death was mercifully quick.

Following a medical examination, warders placed Burnett's body in a coffin and carried it out of the block. After a brief service conducted by Rev. Dickson, Burnett was buried in a prepared grave behind the execution block. The hangman and other prison representatives joined the governor in his office and the warders were permitted to go for their breakfast. Few staff went home for breakfast that day as they were confronted by a large group of protesters at the front gate.

A large mob of around 200 people had gathered to protest against the hanging. They waited for a notice to be displayed giving details of the time the prisoner was executed but no notice was ever published. When the crowds eventually dispersed the staff returned to their duties and the magistrates and other officials left the prison. The remainder of the prisoners returned to work at 10.30am, instead of the customary 8am.

In the 1970s, the building of a new gate complex was sanctioned. The work was completed in 1974 and the new block housed a new female remand unit and a freedom-training hostel. The remaining space was utilised to hold staff rooms and administration offices.

The prison has hit the headlines on various occasions since then due to several highly critical reports. Its swift decline can be traced by quotes from the Chief Inspector of Prisons, Mr Clive Fairweather. In 1997 he praised morale among staff and prisoners but later he condemned the prison as "idle, unsafe and failing". His 2002 report painted a picture of violence and drug abuse within the prison and identified the lack of any meaningful regime. The inspector's 2002 report said that five years previously it had been a well-run establishment with good staff and prisoner morale but since then the prison had "greatly deteriorated" This was due mostly to overcrowding and a rise in the drugs culture in the north-east - resulting in a high level of drug misuse among newly admitted prisoners.

His criticisms prompted a meeting between Scottish Justice Minister Jim Wallace and Prison Governor Audrey Mooney. The staff rejected the inspector's overall assessment, although the prison service accepted most of his recommendations for improvements. Governor Mooney stated there had been many improvements since his visit.

Clive Fairweather's successor agreed with his criticisms. In November 2004, a report into conditions at Craiginches Prison described overcrowding there as "startling". The new Chief Inspector of Prisons, Andrew McLellan, said the situation there was the worst in Scotland. The prison currently houses 250 prisoners in a jail whose capacity is 155.

The Scottish Prison Service explained because Aberdeen takes prisoners directly from the court, it would have higher numbers inside than long-term jails. The service spends one and a half million pounds a week on facilities across Scotland to replace unfit accommodation. But they admitted there was little they could do to increase capacity at Craiginches.

Andrew McLellan insisted that overall his report into Aberdeen was a good one, and praised staff there for their commitment and abilities. But he said overcrowding is a "damaging issue" confronting the jail, and called for courts to find alternatives to jail when sentencing criminals.

The prison's role will continue to be evaluated and assessed. 'Craigie' has served its purpose well but these are turbulent times for the Scottish Prison Service. The criticisms levelled at Craiginches are echoed across all prisons throughout Scotland and, with privatisation a very real proposition, its future is far from certain.

7
The Dee

Up to the late 18th century and early 19th century, Torry didn't feature prominently in the history of Aberdeen. There is very little mention of Torry in the history of the port of Aberdeen. Its location near to the mouth of the harbour meant that it was used mainly as an anchorage for larger ships unable to negotiate the narrow channel of the Dee. Torry had always remained isolated from Aberdeen and the North. Up to this point the only access to Aberdeen had been by boat or ferry. The traveller willing to take a risk would cross the river at the ford at Ruthrieston.

The Old Bridge of Dee was built in the 16th century but it was hardly convenient for the inhabitants of Torry. The bridge had been projected as far back as the 14th century. Bishop William Elphistone began the work and materials, including dressed stone from Morayshire, were imported. Work was suspended when Elphistone died in 1514. Prompted by his successor Gavin Dunbar, work resumed four years later under the guidance of Alexander Galloway and Thomas Franche. Seven ribbed archways supported its flat 4 metre wide roadway. In 1840 John Smith the City Architect widened the bridge. His original plan was to replace the bridge with a new one but the council had rejected his proposal. He removed the facings on the west side and replaced them once he had widened the bridge.

There had been an earlier bridge across the River Dee although its location has never been firmly established. A charter dated 1384 mentions its existence and it's thought the crossing may have spanned the river at Craiglug. However the bridge had fallen into disrepair by the mid 15th century and was never replaced.

In 1850, the Caledonian, Great North of Scotland and North British Railways began to provide rail links to Aberdeen. To help facilitate this, a railway bridge was built to traverse the river. It crossed at a point just south of Craiginches Prison and stretched over to Ferryhill.

The North side of the river became more accessible in 1830 when the

The Wellington Suspension Bridge.
© Aberdeen Library and Information Services

Wellington Suspension Bridge was built. Affectionately known as the "Chain Briggie", it was intended to provide a direct link from the fast expanding city to Kincardineshire. The bridge connected Ferryhill with the high bank of Craiglug eliminating the need for the long hike up the Hardgate to the Bridge of Dee. It was built utilising plans drawn up by city architect John Smith, known locally as 'Tudor Johnny', and Captain Samuel Brown. Smith was also responsible for the pylons and approaches while James Abernethy oversaw the project. Funding was assisted by donations from the Shoemaker Craft and the Aberdeen Hammermen Incorporated Trades. When the bridge first opened it was for pedestrians only but carriage traffic was allowed to cross a year later. Initially a charge of one halfpenny was levied to cross the bridge and a tollbooth was situated on the west side to collect the fee. The toll payment was finally dropped in 1879.

Ambitious plans were proposed to open the area south of Aberdeen for development. The waters of the Dee were a hindrance to these plans and many engineers thought the river could act as a natural scouring agent for the harbour. This would be made possible by diverting the channel of the

The Dee during its diversion. © Aberdeen Library and Information Services

River Dee to a totally engineered and stable bed at the southern edge of the shallow estuary. This would free up an area of 90 acres for expansion on the north side of the river, and allow the progressive southward extension of Market Street.

The procrastination that delayed the project went on for a couple of decades but the growth of steam trawling provided a fresh impetus to the project. The urgent need for expansion of the harbour area led to the end of the squabbling and a decision to divert the Dee was finally taken. The Aberdeen Harbour Act of 1868 allowed the harbour commissioners to divert the river to the south.

Before this plan the course of the River Dee followed a markedly different direction. The river flow up to the Wellington Suspension Bridge was exactly as now, but immediately beyond the bridge its channel ran due north for half a mile following the route of the railway line before veering due east, roughly following the outline of what is now the Albert Basin to Point Law. After that it followed the same course to sea as it does nowadays. A small stream called Scott's Burn split from the main waterway at Craiglug before rejoining the river further upstream. This formed a large fig-shaped piece of land that was frequently under water. There were several of these islands dotted around the area and marked on old maps as 'The Inches'. When the Dee was in spate the overflow found its way to the sea by a channel known as the Spillwater, which emerged south of Point Law.

At one point, a small stream skirting the areas now occupied by Waterloo, Regent and Trinity Quays joined the river. Several small tributaries joined the stream at various points. The Pow, Millburn and Denburn all flowed into the brook, which curved southwards at what is now the junction of Market Street and Guild Street. The watercourse flowed into a wide basin situated at a site roughly between what is now South College Street, Marywell Street and Portland Street. This area of water functioned as Aberdeen's original harbour while fishing vessels landed their catch at a wooden jetty at Point Law.

On the south side of the Dee the whole of the area now forming the Albert Basin was liable to flooding. The area from Point Law to Poynernook Road was frequently submerged due to tidal incursions. These sometimes extended southwards to Wellington Bridge and what is now South Esplanade West. All these areas could be reclaimed after the Dee was diverted.

Work on this mammoth project was undertaken in 1870 and eventually completed three years later. Firstly a dam was built at the southern end of the estuary allowing the new one-mile long channel to be cut into the earth. The weir above Mickle Cairn was removed and an embankment was built across the old channel. After this was completed, the resulting debris excavated from the area was used to fill up the old bed along with material from city landfill sites.

These changes gave the river a more powerful and stable route and paved the way for the harbour to be improved and developed. Quays and wharves were built on both sides of the old river and the Albert Basin was formed. The land reclamation from the estuary permitted the building of Old Ford, Russell, Raik and Stell Roads, the last two being named after the long-established salmon pools located in the old channel of the Dee.

A rather unusual phenomenon occurred towards the end of the 19th century. For a few days in 1895 it was possible to walk across the river. On the 26th January a severe snowstorm began to fall in the Aberdeen area. An intense frost developed over the next few days and large blocks of ice began floating down the river. By the 9th February the

The frozen River Dee proved a great attraction.
© Aberdeen Library and Information Services

'Aberdeen Journal' reported the water had completely frozen over and the river was proving to be a great attraction to the public. Children skated and adults held impromptu parties on the surface over the next few days before a change in the weather caused the ice to thaw.

Incidentally the sport of water polo began on the River Dee around 1863. The Bon Accord Club established an annual challenge between swimmers who lived in Aberdeen. Its purpose was to provide its members with a new, exciting and unique contest. The aim of the game was to pass an inflated pig's bladder through the defence to the opposite bank. The team scoring the most times was declared the winner.

During the 19th century the fish market had been moved three times so a more permanent location was required. Despite pleas from Torry fishermen for a location on the southern side of the estuary, the new Fish Market was built at Commercial Quay in 1889. To gain better access to the south side of the river Market Street was extended and the Victoria Bridge was built. This five-arched stone structure was designed by J. H. Blyth of Edinburgh and built by John Fyfe of Kemnay Quarries.

Earlier, two iron constructions had been rejected in favour of the more classic design using Kemnay granite. The builder offered it to Aberdeen Town Council at a reduced rate to ensure that his stone was used in the project. The town council, the harbour commissioners and the City of Aberdeen Land Association had raised money for the project. The Davidson family of Balnagask also contributed towards the building fund.

The bridge cost £25,000 to build, £6,000 more than was originally estimated. This was mainly because much deeper foundations were required than first envisaged. With its slender piers, rounded cutwaters, and flat segmental arches it is a good example of a late 19th century masonry bridge. The building of the bridge was not without its share of drama, twice during construction the temporary wooden bridge was swept away by strong currents.

The bridge was officially opened on Saturday 2nd July 1881. Large crowds of people lined up along Market Street for the opening ceremony. Flags were displayed along the route and all the ships in the harbour were festooned with bunting. As Lord Provost Esslemont led a deputation across the bridge, the Band of the City Rifle Volunteers played 'Owre the water to Torry'.

Another bridge was set to span the Dee within the next century. The King George VI Bridge was built upstream from the Wellington Suspension Bridge and rail viaduct. Built in 1939, its brief was to provide a more direct route from the new Kincorth Housing schemes to the city centre.

The diversion of the Dee and the harbour re-development led the way for the rapid development of Torry. Its close proximity to the new fish market lead to a rapid influx of people and an area to the south of the river was set aside for housing. The whole area between Point Law on the north side, and Sinclair Road and Wellington Road on the south side, became a thriving centre for the expanding white fish and herring processing industry.

A sizeable proportion of the catch was cold smoked to make kippers and finnan haddock in smoke houses. Fish can be either cold or hot smoked. Cold smoking is the preferred method in Britain. The fish are smoked at temperatures of 85°F (29.5°C), which doesn't cook the fish. It usually takes about 24 hours to produce one batch of cold smoked fish. These establishments were a characteristic feature of Torry and the area around Aberdeen harbour. They used louvered ventilators to draw the smoke from burning wood chips through racks of split and gutted fish.

Many associated industries like ice manufacturing and net making moved into the area so further improvements on the south bank of the river were sanctioned. One million cubic yards of earth was removed at a cost of £51,585. Some land belonging to Torry Farm needed to be purchased. The compensation amount was hotly disputed and was finally resolved at Stonehaven Sheriff Court. Torry Harbour was completed in 1898 and the new Torry Dock joined it several years later.

The arrival of steam trawling led to a revival of the shipbuilding industry. Back in 1741, The Gibbon family owned a small shipyard in Torry. Records indicate they were one of the earliest shipbuilders to operate out of the area. However they eventually moved their yard to Footdee. There followed a period when the industry was absent from the south side of the river. However 1871 seemed to be a golden time for the firm of Leckie, Wood and Munro. They launched two large steamers in that year but by November the firm had closed.

While this was seen as a setback it didn't deter other yards from opening. John Lewis and Sons were located at the west side of the new Torry Dock, while another big firm based itself at Greyhope Road. Following in his grandfather's footsteps, John Duthie opened for business in 1891 and proceeded to exploit the need for new steam drifters and trawlers.

John Duthie prosecuted the shipbuilding business well. The firm's large and spacious yard was ideal for launching ships with slipways leading into the water from Greyhope Road. During a launch the main road was blocked off and temporary slipways were fixed across the road to facilitate easy access to the water. The firm invested heavily in the latest hi-tech machinery that negated the need for heavy manual work. Mobile cranes were moved around the yard on a network of rails. The yard was responsible for a wide variety of vessels from small cargo ships to large trawler / drifters. For several years, the company was building 14 trawlers a year. However the golden years were not to last and shipbuilding went into a steep decline. The last trawler built was the Kinclaven A17 in July 1924. The firm survived until December 1925 when the last ship 'Fire King' was launched.

Several local dignitaries attended a ceremony at Torry Dock on the 4th September 1922. The Anglo-American Oil Company opened a storage and distribution depot for oil and petrol at Mansefield Road. The first tanker to arrive in Torry Dock was the 1000-ton S. S. Juanita. It transferred its cargo by means of an underground pipeline to the four 30-feet high tanks - two for oil and two for petrol. Little did any of the attendees realise this might be an indication of things to come.

In 1965, Shell UK leased 5000 square yards of ground near Torry Harbour to use as a base for their exploration of the North Sea. Additional berthing space for their exploration vessels was also acquired at Maitland's Quay. Geologists were convinced there were large deposits of oil out there and began a programme of tests to find it. The first seismic explosive tests were carried out that year to determine likely areas for exploration. Their efforts paid off and oil was eventually discovered in the North Sea in September 1969.

The arrival of oil businesses hastened the demise of the traditional industries. Oil support vessels replaced trawlers in Torry Dock and, worst of all, the picturesque area of Old Torry was swept away to make way for the various oil bases. In October 1971, the council voted 31 to 3 in favour of scrapping the village.

Many people were outraged at what they regarded as an act of vandalism on the part of the council. Officials maintained the houses were of poor quality and of no great historical value. To be fair the council were probably acting in good faith. The oil boom meant the land near the river was required urgently and this was seen as vital for the economic prosperity of the city.

Feelings about the impending demolition amongst residents were mixed, as there is a vast difference between loving history and living it. While many residents loved the area, they weren't all that keen on the living conditions. The houses had been built on reclaimed land and were subsiding fast. The homes were in urgent need of improvement but restoration costs were prohibitive. Old Torry was finally demolished in 1974.

With the current fervour for conservation at any price, it is doubtful if the council would have received permission to do it now. However examples of the type of housing in Old Torry still survive today. Thankfully the cottages of the fisher square in Abbey Road were outside the development area and therefore escaped demolition. They were built in 1870 and designed by William Smith who was the architect responsible for Balmoral Castle. They were the last houses specifically built for fishermen.

Another bridge spanned the Dee during the early 1980's. Following tradition, this one was also named in honour of the reigning monarch, however this time the sovereign actually attended the opening. Queen Elizabeth II opened the bridge on 15th August 1984. The increase in commercial traffic necessitated the construction of the crossing to the east of the old suspension bridge. Work got underway in April 1981 when contractors A. Monk & Co. began their preliminary excavations. The bridge's construction had been delayed because of wrangles between the regional and the city council over the cost of its granite cladding. Unlike the other bridges that exploited the shortest distance across the river, the three-arched structure was built in an angular direction across the Dee.

The new bridge's sleek design overshadowed its near neighbour and the Wellington Suspension Bridge became a pedestrian walkway. Extensive rebuilding had been undertaken in 1930 and 1987 but "The Chain Briggie" was allowed to fall into disrepair, as no funds were available to restore it. This resulted in the bridge being closed off to the public in the early part of 2001. There are plans to reopen the suspension bridge once sufficient funds have been obtained.

The Dee had been the main reason why Torry had remained isolated for many centuries. Conversely its diversion was the main reason behind Torry's expansion. In the last decade of the 19th century Torry would experience a period of economic growth that was set to continue well into the 20th century. Its days as a sleepy fishing village were well and truly over.

8
Disaster on the Dee

Wednesday 5th April 1876 was a pleasant spring day and a large number of people had flocked south of the River Dee to enjoy a nice day out at the Bay of Nigg. This particular Wednesday had been declared a public holiday to celebrate the Spring Sacramental Fast. For many, the religious aspect of the sacramental fast had ceased to be significant and they grasped the opportunity to have a relaxing day out. Carnival stalls had been erected and the local public houses reported a brisk trade. However what should have been a pleasant excursion was about to become a day that many would never forget. In particular, the people queuing to board the River Dee Ferry were about to become embroiled in a fight for survival.

Torry had always been a popular holiday destination for the people of Aberdeen. Away from the city smoke, they could wander around the Gramps, explore the rocky coves at the Bay of Nigg or visit the Well of St Fittick. The ferry would have been an attractive proposition to the revellers, as a short boat ride would have been infinitely better than a lengthy detour via the Wellington Suspension Bridge. The ferry operators were expecting large amounts of people and had waived concession rates to regular passengers in an effort to reduce numbers. The management also arranged for police to be in attendance to help with crowd control.

The course of the river had only recently been diverted and the ferry plied its trade across the narrowest section of the channel. Its regular route was from Point Law to Ferry Place in Torry. The width of the waterway at the crossing point was only 160 yards but unfortunately on this occasion the river had become swollen. The mild weather had caused snow on the hills to thaw and this sent a rapid current, estimated at six to eight knots per hour, flowing towards the sea.

The ferry was owned by Aberdeen Council and leased to the operators. The relatively inexperienced crew had only been in place for three months. A large new flat-bottomed boat had been purchased from William Hall to cater

The Dee Ferry. © Aberdeen Journals

for increasing demand. The ferry was 25 feet in length, 8 feet 10 inches wide and 2 feet 4 inches in depth and designed to carry 30 passengers or a payload of about 8 tons.

The boat was propelled across the channel by means of a large wire rope secured at each bank of the river. The rope ran along the length of the boat by means of friction rollers at stem and stern and entwined around a fixed wheel. The boatmen moved the ferry by turning the wheel manually. This method of propulsion had proved highly effective, as no problems had occurred up to this point. Nevertheless on this day the swift current had caused anxiety amongst the boatmen, particularly as passenger numbers increased as the day progressed.

With the river in spate it's questionable whether the ferry should have been operating at all. Immediately preceding the ferry's last trip, an ordinary rowing boat crowded with passengers had experienced a difficult journey. The rowboat had made the passage rapidly, although the strength of the current had carried it far down the river.

In the middle of the afternoon, when the tide was almost half-ebb, the ferry began its trip from the Torry side. It was reported that the passengers were particularly anxious to get on board and there seems to have been little effort to prevent overcrowding. As the boat reached the Aberdeen side the impatient crowd swarmed over the fencing at the jetty and forced themselves onto the boat before all those from the other side could disembark.

At this point the crewman in charge of turning the wheel left the boat and disappeared into the crowd. William Masson gave various reasons for leaving his post. He first said he went to fetch a glass of water for his assistant. Later he changed his story and said he went to warn officials about the overcrowding. Several witnesses corroborated Masson's account and stated that Alexander Kennedy, the official in charge, ignored him and continued to take fares. Kennedy stated that he had not heard Masson's protestations and would have acted upon them if he had.

Shortly after three o'clock, the boat began its return trip from Point Law with 76 passengers aboard. The assistant boatman was the only crewmember on board but several passengers helped him turn the wheel. Observers on the bank noted that the boat's progress was slow and that it was sitting low in the water because of the excess weight. They were alarmed to see the gunwale of the boat was only a couple of inches from the water surface.

Alexander Craig, a fisherman from Torry, was convinced it was dangerous for the ferry to cross in these conditions and had shouted across to his wife Jane to advise her to wait until the next trip. His warning went unheeded and the woman scrambled on board. Certain of impending disaster the fisherman launched his boat downstream of the ferry and reached midstream just as disaster struck.

When the ferry was halfway across it began to experience the full force of the current. It was carried so far eastward the wire rope became strained and taut, hindering any further progress. It was impossible to wind the wheel either forwards or backwards. The passengers had remained fairly calm up to this point but a few began to realise the seriousness of the situation. In their panic they caused the ship to list slightly on the west side causing water to flow in. The terrified passengers began to shout for help, as several of them were quickly submerged.

It was thought that the taut rope was causing the ferry to tilt awkwardly and ship water. In an effort to make the boat sit upright in the water a decision was taken to cut the rope. However when this was done the ferry moved with such a jolt it immediately rolled over and capsized. William Smith, who supplied fresh water to shipping, witnessed the boat going over and said it struck the water with the strength of a sledgehammer and was convinced several people were killed instantly.

A handful of passengers who had jumped from the boat immediately prior to the disaster were fortunate because they were swept clear of the crowd and escaped injury when the boat overturned. They were also very lucky when they were able to clamber up the side of the vessel when the strong current swept them back to the wreckage. The remaining passengers were either swept into the swollen river or trapped beneath the upturned shell.

Immediate steps were taken to mount a rescue. Four boats were launched from the Torry side, and one from the Aberdeen end. The second ferry, whose passengers had disembarked just minutes before, quickly joined them. The strong current hampered the rescue attempts. The passengers were swept away to all corners of the river and faced an agonising wait, as the rescuers were not able to concentrate their efforts in one spot.

Alexander Craig, the fisherman who had launched his boat prior to the accident was on hand to rescue several passengers. Fearing for his wife Jane's safety he had reached the boat just as the accident occurred and hauled her from the water. The woman had a miraculous escape as several others in the water had grabbed the creel on her back in desperation. She was in real danger of being strangled as well as drowned but her husband grabbed her just as she went under. It's thought his decision to launch his boat prior to the accident saved at least ten lives

There were several other miraculous tales. Two sisters, Elizabeth and Mary Ann Simpson, had been separated when the boat overturned and each woman had feared the other had been drowned. However boats launched from opposing sides of the bank had picked them up and a tearful reunion was soon arranged. A Mrs Farquhar of Jute Street had clung resolutely to her infant child, who she had been carrying in her arms. Luckily a fisherman's wife at the Torry side grabbed her and the child when the current carried them towards the bank. A father rescued his own daughter. He heard Williamina Strachan's cries of desperation, saw her floating seawards and managed to reach her.

George Hogg was one of a party of five shoemakers who were on board to "enjoy a day of music" at Nigg Bay. He and the rest of his workmates jumped clear of the boat into the river and steadily made for the south bank. George was a disabled man who walked with the aid of a crutch. Halfway to the shore he accidentally let go of his crutch and swam back to retrieve it. The second trip exhausted him and he only just managed to pull himself, and his crutch, onto the bank. After the ordeal, he quipped with rescuers that he lost his flute and would have to go back in to get it. Understandably he had sought to relieve a tense situation with humour. However his jubilant mood was tempered when he was told of the death of one of his colleagues. Archibald Duncan had been pulled unconscious from the river but all attempts to revive him had failed.

Unfortunately there were many other tales of tragedy. George Selbie had boarded the ferry with his sister Margaret. He tried vainly to save her but missed her in the confusion and brought another girl ashore instead. One small consolation for George was that he managed to save a valuable family heirloom; he placed his father's gold watch in his mouth when the boat capsized and it remained there throughout his ordeal. A young boy was within sight of the Torry shoreline and was only a few strokes away from safety. Suddenly he began to struggle, apparently overcome by cold or cramp. A Footdee fisherman called Walker made a desperate bid to grasp him as he went under. For a brief second the man thought he had managed to grab his head, unfortunately he only caught the boy's cap.

All in all, 32 people lost their lives that day. Amongst the victims were brothers Andrew and George McKilliam, aged 17 and 14 respectively. George Dickie, a stonecutter from Nelson Street, left a widow and three young children. He'd refused to board an earlier boat as he thought it was too crowded. Then there was James Munro, a 40-year-old foundry labourer, who was on board with his new wife. When the boat capsized he held firmly on to her hand for some minutes before relaxing his grip. She managed to grab hold of the upturned hull but he was washed away.

The youngest female fatality was 13-year old Jessie McCondach, a message girl from Little Belmont Street; She'd been one of those unfortunate passengers who were unable to disembark when the crowd rushed to get on at Point Law. The youngest person to die was 10-year old William Duncan, who stayed with his mother at Stronach Court, Exchequer Row. When his body was recovered he still had his return fare clasped firmly in his right hand.

The death toll would have been much higher if it weren't for the team of rescuers and their prompt action. The salmon fishers launched their flotilla of boats promptly and were responsible for rescuing several passengers. James Brown, the mate of the schooner 'Speed', garnered many plaudits. He had been cruising on the river with his family when the accident happened. With the help of two bystanders he managed to rescue five people. James Mowat, a member of the Dee Swimming Club, dived under the water several times in an attempt to find people. Unfortunately his attempts failed because of the murkiness of the water.

The swollen waters eventually subsided but it was several days before all the bodies were recovered. "Creepers" used in trawling were deployed to help, these devices were long metal rods with cords attached bearing numerous hooks. Twenty trawlers lined up between Point Law and Abercrombie Jetty and began the grim task of searching the water. The deceased's belongings were displayed at the Roundhouse for identification purposes while the bodies were interned at the local police station.

A relief fund for the relatives was launched and a considerable amount of money was raised. A pamphlet called 'Catastrophe on the River Dee' was published on the day after the disaster, the proceeds of which were donated to the appeal. Several local poets were inspired to break into verse and offer their view of the situation. Police Sergeant William Shelley's work 'Are there any bodies found?' helped to boost the relief fund considerably. However there were several other authors with a more political motive in mind. Arthur Mitchell's prophetic poem entitled 'A Brig to Torry' pointed the finger at the local politicians whose procrastinations had delayed such a structure to be built.

In the days following the disaster there was much recrimination and many allegations of blame were thrown about. Many thought the police were culpable for not supervising the situation properly. The ferry management were heavily criticised for cutting corners and there was even a sizeable contingent that thought the impatient passengers were ultimately responsible for their own fate.

A Board of Trade enquiry into the circumstances of the disaster was instigated a fortnight after the tragedy. A scant amount of new information was gained by this enquiry, as much of it had been evident at the time of the disaster. The Board of Trade heavily criticised the efficiency of the ferry management team. Several members of the crew had expressed concerns over safety but these warnings had largely gone unheeded.

On the final day of the enquiry Alexander Kennedy, the ferry leaseholder emphatically stated he had not noticed the boat was overcrowded and wouldn't have allowed the crew to cast off if he did. He also claimed that the police in attendance had failed to keep the crowds at bay. However he conceded that he had not given direct instructions to the policemen on how to prevent overcrowding, assuming that they would know how to proceed if the situation occurred.

It was revealed that the ferryboat used was highly unsuitable for use in the new channel. Several witnesses thought that the wire method of propulsion was incompatible with the stronger currents caused by the river's new course. In their opinion an oar driven vessel would have been a more suitable alternative. The state of the wire also caused some concern and may have hindered the progress of the boat. On examination, the rope had not been spliced but laid over and kept in place by some spun yarn instead.

The Victoria Bridge pictured in 1881.
© Aberdeen Library and Information Services

Enquiries revealed the crew had done it themselves several days previously rather than consult a rigger.

Remarkably a similar disaster was narrowly averted just a few months later. The Torry ferryboat, now propelled by oars, was swept downstream during a fierce gale in November 1876. Luckily the boat was grounded on the Torry bank and there were no casualties.

Plans for a new bridge across the Dee had been mooted as far back as 1868 but these proposals had frequently foundered. City officials had expressed fears that a bridge at this location might develop a rival municipality across the river and constantly rejected the proposal. Ironically the City of Aberdeen Land Association had instigated the latest of these bids on the day prior to the disaster. This time the association proposed a joint venture but the council rejected the offer again.

However the huge public outcry following the disaster gave the shelved plans a fresh impetus and the sheer weight of public opinion forced the

71

councillors to rethink their plans. As a direct result the Victoria Bridge was built in 1881. The new bridge proved to be highly popular and was a significant factor in Torry's rapid expansion in the late 19th century. For a while the ferry coexisted alongside its replacement but gradually the trips were phased out and boat trips across the Dee were consigned to history.

The incident was widely reported at the time and became known as Aberdeen's Black Fast Day". Yet in the ensuing years the tragedy was largely forgotten and many inhabitants of Torry were unaware of the disaster. However a plaque commemorating the event was unveiled at the city end of the Victoria Bridge in February 2005. Local dignitaries along with thirty pupils from Walker Road Primary School attended the touching ceremony. The children, dressed in Victorian clothes and each carrying a placard bearing the name of one of the victims, marched across the bridge led by the city drummer. They stood silently during the ceremony as the tale of Torry's darkest day was related to them.

It's fitting that the Victoria Bridge now bears a memorial to the disastrous event that led to its creation. Hopefully now the victims who lost their lives that day will not be treated as a tragic footnote in the history of Aberdeen

9
Religion

Fishermen are notoriously superstitious and certain actions were considered highly unlucky. Spitting on deck would curse the ship and whistling would summon up a gale. Certain words were outlawed too; salmon was constantly referred to as "red fish". Salt was never mentioned at sea but the wives would sprinkle their men with it before casting off. It was also considered unlucky to turn a vessel against the sun or sail on a Sunday. Cats were feared because of their association with witches and the sight of a rabbit was enough to cancel a fishing trip.

Certain men and women were also regarded as unlucky. Occasionally there might be no obvious reason for this but frequently this might be because the person had a physical deformity. One such individual who was considered "ill fitted" was Ladles Meg. She worked in a fish house in Sinclair Road and although she was quite harmless, was always keenly avoided on sailing days.

It was fairly common for the men to send their women to their boats first to see if any undesirables were in the vicinity. Even in these more enlightened times it is considered bad luck to meet a minister before sailing. To even mention the word 'minister' at sea was considered a portent of doom and disaster. Despite this, the seafarers regarded religion as a deeply significant part of their lives and the fisher folk of Old Torry were no exception. If any person took the Lord's name in vain it would be immediately met with a resounding chorus of "caul' iron". Touching iron was thought to counteract the bad luck.

The patron saint of the area is known by many names. Surprisingly locals often referred to him in past times as Sandy Fittick. He is referred to in different journals as Saint Mofutacus, Saint Fiacre, Saint Mufott and Saint Fittick. The latter is the most common and has given its name to many landmarks in the area, so for continuity purposes this is the version we'll settle for.

Saint Fittick was an Irish monk spreading the gospel in Europe. While in France he had a vision, in which he was ordered to get to the coast and board the first ship bound for the north. While at sea, a great storm blew up off the coast at Nigg. The superstitious sailors blamed the holy man and threw him overboard. He was washed ashore exhausted and near to death. The salt water he'd swallowed made him thirsty. The legend pronounces as he prayed for water, a little spring bubbled up from under his hand and his life was saved. He settled in the area and continued to preach the gospel to locals for the rest of his life.

The well, it was claimed, had miraculous therapeutic powers and drew pilgrims from afar for centuries. After the Reformation the practice was denounced as superstitious heathenism. People desperate for a cure persisted in visiting the well and risked the wrath of the Church. Those who were caught seeking cures at the holy well were fined heavily. St. Fittick's Well is still there but now, because of erosion, its waters bubble up into the sea.

Before the Reformation, a statue of the Virgin Mary stood on the bridge over the drainage-channel and funeral parties coming to St. Fittick's Church from Cove or Skateraw (Newtonhill) would stop, uncover their heads and bow their heads in prayer. This ritual lasted well into the 19th century. No one remembered the statue by that time, yet the tradition continued.

St. Fittick's Kirk is a roofless ruin standing on an open site overlooking the Bay of Nigg. The church's antiquity rivals the much larger and more important Aberdeen medieval churches of St Nicholas and St Machar. The Church of St. Fittick is first mentioned in a charter of 1189-1199 that refers only to the 'ecclesiam de nig' (church of Nigg). Early records show that David de Bernham, the then Bishop of St. Andrews, dedicated the original church of St. Fittick in 1242. The second St. Fittick's Kirk was built on the same site and originates from the 17th century. It is widely thought that parts of the original building were incorporated into the new structure during construction.

However the site may have had religious connections prior to the church's dedication, as there is evidence of a wattle and daub structure standing on

St. Fittick's Church today. © Gordon Bathgate

the site prior to the 13th century. It possibly started off as a votive shrine where people gave thanks for the well's cures. To the casual observer the church may seem to be positioned in an odd location. The Kirk is situated halfway up the hill and lies at an angle from the main road. One might think that the top of the hill might have been a more logical spot for it but the church's location can be attributed to a part of the landscape no longer in existence. It's thought that the original structure was built at the waterside of an old lagoon that dried up centuries ago. A charter dated 1233 refers to the land near the church as 'stagnis' or boggy. The ruins stand on grounds originally owned by the Abbey of Arbroath. The Abbots held the church until the Reformation.

St. Fittick's Church preached Catholicism for over 300 years. At the time of the Reformation the Church of Scotland broke away from the structure of the Church of Rome and 'reformed' the worship and administration of the faith. In Scotland this reformed faith moved towards a Calvinist and Presbyterian system.

During the Reformation, religious extremists from the south arrived in

Aberdeen to stir up trouble. Churches, monasteries and convents were attacked and destroyed and looting was widespread. One looter stripped the lead and the bells from St. Machar's Cathedral. He loaded up his ship and set sail for Holland. He didn't get far as the ship was wrecked on Girdleness and he went down with his plunder.

The Reformation didn't seem to affect local parishioners much and the new radical religious ideals were largely ignored, although a reformed minister was eventually appointed in 1567. St. Fittick's Church continued to be Episcopalian until 1716 when Presbyterianism became the chosen creed.

This move in faith had been forced upon the parishioners because they supported the Stewart dynasty during the 1715 rebellion. The then minister Richard Maitland was removed from his post after 42 years for praying for the Old Pretender. He was obviously well liked as the east gable is dated 1704 with the initials 'RM' inscribed in memory of him.

The ruins of the church provides several other clues to its chequered past. Above the church, the old weather vane is dated 1763. The remains of the badly weathered belfry can be seen at the top the east gable. Its bell would toll to warn villagers from Burnbanks, Cove and Downies, as well as from Torry, that a service was about to start. The bell was made by John Mowat of Old Aberdeen and was inscribed: "Sabata Pango Funra Plango". Translated from the Latin, this reads, "Sabbaths I proclaim, Funerals I toll."

A small watchtower stands in the northeast corner of the churchyard. This was built in the 1820s to deter body snatchers, as the grim practice of stealing bodies from graveyards was commonplace then. 'Resurrectionists' would sell them to medical students for dissection and the churchyard's isolated location made it a prime target for this deplorable offence.

The first incident of this kind took place at the church on Christmas Day 1808, when the body of 90-year-old widow Mrs. Janet Spark was stolen. It's believed the body snatchers were interrupted and they fled rapidly with their newly acquired possession. In their haste they left behind a spade with the name 'Rae' etched on the handle. Suspicion immediately fell upon a local medical student who promptly fled the country. Mrs. Spark's naked corpse was washed up on the Bay of Nigg six weeks later. The two students had buried her body in a sand bank at the north end of the bay, intending to return for it once the fuss had died down. However a great storm blew up along the northeast coat and swept the body out to sea.

These events caused widespread alarm across the area and a mort stone was obtained in an effort to allay the fears of the community. Superintendent Gibb of the Aberdeen Harbour Works donated the large polished stone block to St. Fittick's in 1816. It cost 2s 6d to transport the stone by cart from the ferry landing point to the church. The heavy slab, which took about four men to move, was placed across each fresh grave to deter the body snatchers from their objective. This made the gruesome task extremely difficult for the resurrectionists, unless they came mob handed.

There are many gruesome tales but in the interests of good taste I'll only recount one more. In 1874, two skeletons were found in ground beside Jessie Petrie's Inn, which used to stand at the foot of Ferry Road. Several months earlier two body snatchers were discovered in the act and fled towards the river. Fearing they were about to be caught they hid the bodies behind the inn and were unable to return for them. This despicable trade ended in 1832 when Warburton's Anatomy Act made it legal for medical students to acquire bodies for dissection.

In the north wall, beside the built-up doorway where the priest's entered, there are signs of what appears to be a leper's window, more commonly known as a leper's squint. This is where the poor unfortunates would gather for spiritual guidance. From here the lepers could take part in the service from outside without alarming the rest of the congregation. The identification of this window is uncertain, as there would have been no lepers in Aberdeen in the 17th or 18th centuries, when the church was rebuilt. However there was a sizeable leper community in the area during previous centuries and the builders may have incorporated it within the new design.

Leprosy affected rich and poor alike. The victims were cast out from the community and left to roam the Tullos Valley. Here they were more or less left to their own devices to forage for food. Occasionally provisions were sent out to them from the leper house in Nelson Street. In a rare act of compassion, the city fathers passed a ruling that stated one peat out of every load that entered the city, had to be yielded to the leper community.

On the south wall beside the doorway, there are rusty chain links that are the remains of the "Jougs", also known as the Scold's Bridle. The bridle fitted over the head and had an apparatus that pierced the tongue if speech were even attempted. The victim was chained to the wall by the church door and was constantly ridiculed by the passing parishioners. Attendance at the church was compulsory, so there was sure to be a fair-sized congregation. Other punishments handed out by the church courts were imprisonment in the steeple, confinement under the vestry, exposure in sackcloth on the high or low repentance stool or flogging at a stake in the churchyard.

During the Scottish War of Independence, Edward the First marched northwards, leaving troops at strategic towns and fortresses behind him. William Wallace, a master of Guerrilla tactics, followed behind him and with his superior force, picked off most of these garrisons. When Edward himself moved on from Aberdeen, he left a strong detachment holding the castle to keep the town out of 'rebel' hands. When Wallace attacked, the English panicked and fled.

It's rumoured that part of William Wallace's body is buried in the southeast corner of the churchyard. After Wallace's execution his body was quartered and sent to different parts of the country. Parts were sent to Berwick-on-Tweed, Perth, Newcastle and Aberdeen. One of his limbs was displayed above the Justice Port in Aberdeen. Under cover of the night, patriots in Aberdeen spirited the arm south of the river to its final resting place in the churchyard at St. Fittick's. However stories like this have surfaced at different places around the country and it's fair to say that St. Fitticks has no more firm evidence to lay claim to the legend than any other location.

There are over 200 headstones in the graveyard, the earliest is dated 1619 and has the initials J. C. inscribed on it. Several prominent locals are buried in the cemetery. These include James Calder, a local merchant. When he died in 1832 he bequeathed over £1000 to the poor of the area. His daughter, Mrs Mary Emslie, is also buried there. She provided funds to repair the kirkyard walls and went on to open a hospital for orphan girls in Albyn Place. It is also the last resting place for several members of the eminent Gibbon family.

Sadly the church began to fall into disrepair under the ministry of the Rev. David Cruden. In 1826, his successor, Rev. Alex Thom took steps to have a new church built on a more convenient site for the parish. Rev. Thom, who had been headmaster of Gordon's Hospital, performed the last service on the 31st May 1829.

It's widely believed that the old baptismal font was removed and presented to Marischal College in 1885. This particular font was later displayed in Provost Skene's House but there is some uncertainty as to its origin. St. Fittick's does in fact contain another early font, which sits on a plinth under a window in the north wall of the church.

While it's not possible to accurately date the year the Kirk was built, it is possible to pinpoint the date of origin of the old manse that stood adjacent to the churchyard. The manse was constructed in 1759 and eventually demolished in 1964. Since the last minister left, it had been used as a private residence and was still in use after World War II. A recent archaeological excavation uncovered its driveway, garden wall and farm buildings. Several clues were also found that indicate a previous building stood on the site and further excavations may provide further hints to its purpose.

The church serves as a significant reminder of the area's history and was the origin of many street names. Farquhar Road is named after an 18th century minister of St. Fittick's who was well known for banging heads together. James Farquhar was a large, fierce man who would often resort to direct physical means to enforce his viewpoint. When two Episcopalian men tried to prevent the first Presbyterian service from happening by beating up the bell ringer: Farquhar charged in, fists flying, and knocked the two men out single-handedly.

The new church of Nigg opened on 7th June 1829 and was designed by architect John Smith. The rectangular stone-built church was of gothic design with a square tower at the west. Located originally in the county of Kincardine, the church was built overlooking the Vale of Tullos. The heritors also partly financed the Wellington Suspension Bridge and were also responsible for the turnpike road between Torry and the Loch of Loirston. The graveyard has one modern extension at the top of which is a war memorial commemorating those lost from the Parish of Nigg. Unfortunately the church building has recently been closed and sold but the future of the graveyard seems secure for the foreseeable future.

It was the duty of the churches in the area to care for the poor and sick. In 1793, records show that 25 people needed help, either permanently or occasionally. Nigg was in a better position to help than others, thanks to endowments producing nearly £50 interest per year. The Reverend Richard Maitland had set up this fund with an initial payment of £27.77. Collections at communion and private donations helped to swell the coffers, as well as other moneymaking services. One of these schemes was the hire of the Mort Cloth, a piece of material used to drape over the coffin at a funeral.

Members of the Kirk Session were responsible for handing out donations. Once expenses were deducted, the balance would be spread amongst the poor and the needy. This was on the strict understanding that, on death, the deceased's property passed back to the poor fund. A disaster at sea would undoubtedly impose a heavy strain on finances. In 1790, six men were lost at sea leaving five widows and 25 children destitute. Collections were made around the area and a sum of £131 was raised. This amount helped to train the children in industry. Sadly this kind of event was all too common.

The local minister launched a savings scheme to help fishermen in their old age. Each man paid 12.5p initially and then an annual fee of 5p thereafter. The funds were supplemented by private donations and totalled £170 after a decade, producing £11 interest annually. Each old man received ten shillings every six months while widows received seven shillings. The care of the poor ceased to be the sole responsibility of the church when the parochial boards were formed in 1845.

In addition to the parochial board, there were other sources where the poor could turn too in time of need. Friendly Societies were private organisations supported by members who contributed a regular sum of money to provide an income in old age or insurance against sickness or inability to work. They became increasingly popular in the 18th and 19th centuries and Torry had its fair share of them. These included the Rechabites, the Shepherds, the Court Wellington Forester's Lodge and the rather curiously named Caledonian Order of Oddfellows.

In 1895, there was an important change in the administration of the poor laws in Scotland. The old parochial board system gave way to new parish councils. The old system was considered to be too harsh on the very people it was trying to help. John Leiper the shoemaker was elected as the first parish councillor and was replaced at the end of his term by James Pope. Pope had recently re-entered public life following a two year tenure as Torry's first town councillor. After a second term as parish councillor he was appointed chairman of both East and West Poorhouses.

The Free Church of Scotland is a Presbyterian Church adhering in its doctrine and worship to the position adopted by the Church of Scotland at the reformation. In 1843, the Church of Scotland was split in two by an event that came to be known as the Disruption. This happened because of a divide between those who maintained that the lairds should have the right to choose the ministers and those who felt it was up to congregations to decide this.

In 1842, after many years of dissension the General Assembly drew up a Claim of Right and presented it to the government. The Kirk maintained they had complete spiritual independence and the state had no right to interfere in such matters. The government refused to accept this and so at the General Assembly of 1843 a walk out took place and the Free Church of Scotland was formed.

At the time of the Disruption, the Free Church was established in Torry. Dr Spence of St. Clement's Church, Footdee was tasked by the Aberdeen Presbytery to get the plan underway. He acted swiftly and with the assistance of divinity students, erected a wooden building on the Torry side of the River Dee. It stood between Bank Street and Pierhead and cost £40 to build.

The congregation grew over a number of years so eventually there was a need for larger premises. In 1865, the congregation moved to a church in Sinclair Road, formerly known as Church Street. This new building was capable of seating 250 people. However even this church was too small for the ever-growing congregation and in 1890 a new church was built in Victoria Road.

The early 20th century was a time of consolidation within different ministries. In 1900 the Free Church united with the United Presbyterian Church to form the United Free Church of Scotland. Then the United Free Church & the Church of Scotland combined in 1929. At this point, approximately 130 members of this congregation decided to form Torry United Free Church. At first they met in The Central Mission Hall in Sinclair Road, while a new building was erected in Grampian Road.

On December 11th 1931, a crowd of 800 people stood patiently in the pouring rain as the opening ceremony was performed. The architect Mr W Gauld handed a decorative key to the widow of a former minister of Torry. Mrs Alex. Murray of Birnham unlocked the door and declared the church open. The Rev. A Johnston Millar, Moderator Elect of The United Free Church (Continuing) performed the dedication service to a packed congregation. Several people who attended had travelled from places as far as Orkney and Wishaw.

The breakaway church quickly progressed and a number of community initiatives were established. The Girls' Guildry and the Boys' Brigade were started to provide activities for the area's youngsters. The Revival Hour was introduced on Saturday evenings as an outreach meeting.

The new church flourished but the old one hit hard times. When the new church opened, the Torry Church in Victoria Road had continued with Church of Scotland services until it finally closed its doors after 148 years in service. The last service was held on Sunday 26th May 1991 and the building is now used as a crèche.

With the influx of new residents to the area in the late 19th century, the demand for churches and other places of worship grew. Work on St. Fittick's Church in Walker Road began on Saturday 19th November 1898 when Lauchlan McKinnon, the convener of the Aberdeen Church Extension Association, laid the foundation stone. Unfortunately he did not live to see the completion of the project.

The church opened one year later on the 24th November 1899. So far the project had cost £2000 and only the first portion of the church had been finished with seating for 550 worshippers. Once completed the church provided accommodation for a further 300 people at an additional charge of £1,100. The architect in charge of the development was Arthur H. L. Mackinnon. It started off as a Chapel of Ease and gained full parish status in 1914. After the closure of Torry Church, the two congregations unified and became Torry St. Fittick's Church.

Many of the fishermen who moved into the area in at the advent of steam trawling were Episcopalians. A mission hall was leased in 1882 for the annual fee of £20. The hall was opened on January 28th 1883 at a ceremony attended by the Bishop of Brechin. In 1893 they erected a church in Victoria Road called St. Peter's Scottish Episcopal Church. This was due in no small part to William Disney Innes, a lay preacher who was ordained in 1896.

As a symbol of the close relationship between the church and the fishing community, the new congregation commissioned a boat. The 'A153 St Peter and St. Andrew' was a rather unusual vessel, as it was never put to sea. Instead she hung from the roof of the church. This was no model, but a 15-foot long, two-masted yawl. The boat cost approximately £22.50 and was built at James Cordiner's yard on the banks of the Dee.

Eventually the church had to be sold because of crippling heating costs and was converted into flats for the elderly. The congregation now worship in the refurbished hall situated at the rear of the old church. The boat found a new home in the vestibule at St. Peters church in Fraserburgh.

The Sacred Heart Roman Catholic Church in Grampian Road has served members of the Catholic community since the 19th November 1911. Charles

The Salvation Army parade down Victoria Road. © Aberdeen Journals

Menart of Glasgow designed the building while local builder David Weir handled the stone and brickwork. The method of masonry work adopted attracted much attention at the time. The stones of Clinterty granite were laid in a "random bed" in all directions. There were no square blocks used in the construction and each stone was fitted in as work proceeded. With the addition of red tiles the effect was quite striking. The style had been in vogue several centuries before but was quite unusual at the time. The church was designed to hold 350 worshippers and cost £4000 to build.

In September 2006, it was revealed that the Sacred Heart Church faces an uncertain future, as the building is too expensive to refurbish. The parishioners have launched a fundraising bid to try to save the church but a spokesman for the Diocese of Aberdeen said it looked likely it would be shut. If the closure goes ahead worshippers would have to use the nearby Scottish Episcopal Church.

Other places of worship included the Victoria Hall in Victoria Road. This was built by subscriptions from a number of local people. The church is not governed by any central organisation but the members work closely with other churches in the area. The first meeting was held on 27th May 1900 in the basement of the building that used to be the Co-op in Victoria Road. The group moved to a small hall in South Esplanade West in 1902. The current building at 107 Victoria Road was first used on the 13th October 1928.

The Salvation Army operates out of premises in Glenbervie Road. The organisation still serves the people of Torry with a range of evangelical and social services today. Although church attendances are steadily declining and its influence in the neighbourhood has diminished, there is still a considerable religious community in the area.

10
Torry's Rapid Expansion

Prior to the 19th century, Torry didn't figure prominently among the fishing villages around Aberdeen. It was just another community nestling close to Aberdeen Harbour. However it is precisely because of its location that Torry was about to experience a period of unparalleled growth.

In the early 1800s, Aberdeen was fast becoming a busy fishing port. Vast amounts of people were attracted to the city because of the boom in steam trawling. This prompted plans to open the area south of Aberdeen for development and Torry was to play a vital role in the city council's plans for expansion.

Torry's large influx of population came mainly from fishing villages in the south but there was one notable exception. Collieston was a thriving fishing community to the north of the River Don. Records show that, at the end of the 19th century, some 165 men were working 63 fishing boats from the village. This prosperity led to the construction of Collieston Pier in 1894.

Ironically, it was the building of the pier that led to the harbour silting up. Small herring boats soon became obsolete and the young men left to join larger boats. By the early 20th century there were not enough men left in the village to haul the large line boats up the beach and the local economy nose-dived. Soon the trickle of men leaving Collieston became a torrent as the population flooded into the now more prosperous Torry.

However Collieston and Torry still retained close links and some villagers maintained a house in both communities. This strong bond led to the introduction of a regular bus service between the two locations. Alex Ross ran a regular bus service from Collieston to Aberdeen. He would drive the bus to Aberdeen in the morning, drive the bus back to Collieston again in the evening and then motorcycle back to his home in Newburgh.

At regular intervals Alex would drive his bus over to Torry, load furniture onto the roof rack of the bus and drive the families and their belongings back to their homes in Collieston where they would spend their holidays. This

Victoria Road. © Aberdeen Library and Information Services

service ran from the early 1920's to the late 1940's when Alex eventually sold the business to Sutherlands of Peterhead.

Collieston's close ties to Torry were broken a long time ago. Both villages' fates were sealed because of the changes to the fishing industry in the late 19th century. Collieston's fortunes declined swiftly while Torry, by virtue of its location, was able to take full advantage of new opportunities.

Initial attempts were made to buy the 115-acre Torry Farm Estate in 1869. However these negotiations fell through because of the inability of the council to reach an agreement. This proved to be a very expensive blunder as they were initially offered the entire estate for just £28,000. The council refused to pay that amount and after long and protracted discussions eventually purchased 31 acres for £20,000. In 1901 the City Fathers purchased another 7 acres for a further payment of £56,500. This must count as one of the biggest financial gaffes ever made by Aberdeen Town Council. The principal objector to buying the Torry Farm Estate was Lord Provost Alexander Nicol. His reticence cost him his municipal seat and he was ousted after just one term in office.

The area, together with Old Aberdeen and Woodside, was incorporated into Aberdeen's boundaries in 1891. There had been considerable opposition to Torry being integrated within the auspices of the city council. Torry had voted overwhelmingly against incorporation in 1890, a poll taken on the 27th September revealed that only 58 ratepayers were in favour while 289 were against incorporation. The new Aberdeen citizens were incensed when the ward was limited to only one representative. Torry's first councillor was James Pope, a local granite merchant. Local fish merchant William Meff, who was largely responsible for Torry gaining its harbour, eventually became the second councillor.

The area around the River Dee became the centre of the fish processing industry and a large number of businesses moved into the area. Benefiting from the rise of fish processing and its ancillary businesses, Torry began to prosper and grow. At the turn of the century it was estimated that nearly 6000 people were employed in either the fish or shipbuilding industries.

Attracted by the promise of prosperity and employment, thousands of fishermen and their families moved into the area. The development came slowly at first. In 1838 the first roads to be given names were Fore Close and Back Close, built on land reclaimed from the estuary. They journeyed from the small villages dotted around the North Sea coast and from as far away as the North of England. Between the years 1881 and 1891, the population of Torry grew to nearly 3000. Within the next 10 years that figure had more than trebled. In 1914, at the outbreak of the First World War, Aberdeen was the biggest fishing port in Britain.

Other types of industry also flourished, albeit briefly. The whaling industry was represented by the Greenland Company who operated a boiling plant on Torry Pier. William Fiddes and Cordiner's Sawmills opened yards to build wooden boxes for the transportation of fish. Cordiner's Victoria Sawmills was originally steam-powered. Marshall of Gainsborough built the single-cylinder horizontal steam engine. A boiler, fired by sawdust and other wood waste from the mill, provided the steam for this engine. The engine was eventually replaced but retained as a standby, and was still in running order in 1977

There were four granite polishing yards belonging to James Pope, Cruickshank, Dawson and Anderson, respectively. Marshall & Co opened their provisions factory, Duncan's established their cooperage, and Harpers opened their foundry and ironworks at Craigshaw. Then there was Barking Geordie's yard where he boiled bark in vats as a preservative for fishing lines against the corrosive nature of salt water.

To accommodate the large influx of families it was decided that tenements would be built near to the fish processing industry on the south side of the river. The City of Aberdeen Land Association had purchased land on the southern side of the Dee Estuary and proceeded to build on it. Old Torry had been situated on the riverside, east of the brickworks. Building work was to take place on the northern slopes of Torry Hill. The first new houses were built in 1883 at 104 and 110 Victoria Road. Calder Duncan and David Alexander built them when their former homes had been demolished to make way for the Duthie Park. The feu charters were dated 1st February, but others followed quickly.

One of the first casualties was the Torry Farm estate. The Torry Farmhouse once stood in the vicinity of the junction of Victoria Road and Menzies Road. Dr. Thomas White Ogilvie described the rapid change in his Book of St. Fittick, published in 1903. In his usual flamboyant style of prose he wrote: -

"On the northern slope of this ridge, where but yesterday stood a decaying farm-house with its "green mantled pool," overhung by old willow trees, there stands to-day a new town, with spacious streets, high buildings, and a bustling traffic; a transformation as rapid and complete as if, but lately, the wonderful Lamp of Aladdin had been rubbed up in Old Torry Farm".

The last owner of Torry farm was William Duncan and when his smallholding was sold he transferred his tenancy to Craiginches Farm. Sadly for Mr Duncan, this farm would also be a casualty to the inexorable march of progress during the 20th century.

Alexander Anderson, a former Lord Provost, was the owner of the Torry and Craiginches estates. He sold them to the City of Aberdeen Land Association for £29,000. As Anderson was also a founding member of the association this enterprise earned him a tidy profit. However to suggest his sole purpose for the new development was for self-gain would be disingenuous. Without his vision and foresight many of Aberdeen's development plans would not have come to fruition.

The new tenements that were built provided a vastly different environment to the traditional cottages of Old Torry. Keen to avoid the mistakes made in the city centre slums, the estate was designed to be spacious with the added provision of underground sewers. In 1899 the sewage from Torry and the west-end of Aberdeen was carried 62 feet under the Dee by a tunnel measuring 342 feet and 8.5 feet externally. The sewer ran from Skene Street, through Golden Square and Point Law. The sewage was then passed through another tunnel under St. Fittick's Hill before being discharged into the sea at the Bay of Nigg.

The depth of the sewers below the surface varied from 12 to 28 feet and at some locations, including Girdleness, huge engineering works cut through 40,000 tons of rock. The chamber that regulated the flow of sewage to the sea was located in an old quarry that supplied the stone that built Girdleness Lighthouse. The valve house, built in 1906, had an automatic tidal flap that prevented the sea from backing up the sewer, but opened when the pressure from the sewage was greater than that of the sea. Seawater could be allowed in to flush out the sewer system. The total length of the main sewer was 3 miles and took 7 years to complete.

The old outfall is still in use but nowadays it is only used as a storm overflow. A longer outfall tunnel at the Nigg Sewage Treatment Plant replaced it in 1988. Four main sewage pipes now meet in a convergent chamber under the middle of St Fittick's Park before passing into the plant.

New Torry was to be socially mixed with working class tenements in the lower half and first class housing further up the hill. Old familiar landmarks such as the old brickworks and Torry Farm disappeared and soon tenements stretched along both sides of the road towards Old Torry. The tall tenements of New Torry were in stark contrast to the cottages of Old Torry. Walker Road, Menzies Road and Sinclair Road, were laid out from 1882 onwards. The grey granite tenements of two and three storeys, with gables at the wall-head and dormer windows line the streets. The low walls around the front gardens once held cast-iron railings that were donated to the war effort in the 1940s.

An ordnance survey map, dated 1900, shows the first houses had already been built on Grampian Road and a similar map from 12 years later reveals that homes had since been built on both sides of it. That 1912 map also reveals the first developments on Oscar Road and Glenbervie Road. Although infinitely better than their city slum counterparts, these new houses still left much to be desired. The kitchen area was just an alcove leading off from the main living area and every tenant had to share the communal toilet with his or her neighbour.

The growing community required a supporting infrastructure and soon schools and shops appeared. The first shops appeared on the left hand side of Victoria Road, near to the corner of Sinclair Road. These included the bakery business of W. G. B. Black and Andrew Noble the grocer. Other well-known retail establishments included James Patton the chemist in Victoria Road and R V Matthews the butcher who retained premises in Menzies Road.

A look at some of the advertisements of the time provides an indication of the wide variety of retail outlets available in Torry. The vast majority of shops advertised 'shipping supplied' but quite a few boasted rather unusual strap lines. The owners of the Victoria Studio proudly embraced new technology by offering new colour photography available in 'up to 16 colours'. They offered the patrons 'photography by electric light at any time, day or night'. J & J Duncan offered bicycles at prices from £1 upwards while Wallace and Milne proudly boasted they had the best possible medicines at moderate and reasonable prices. Milne's Restaurant offered customers their 'famed mutton pies', and who could resist "the pickled tongues and salt beef always on hand" from Alexander G. Strachan?

The Kirkhill Dairy on St. Fitticks Road served Torry with fresh milk daily. This was in the days before sterilised, pasteurised milk was delivered in bottles to the doorstep. The delivery boys would collect the flagons and containers from the houses and take them back to the horse drawn cart, where they were filled with fresh milk from the large churns.

The Aberdeen roll or buttery, better known locally as a rowie, is a popular delicacy up and down the east coast of Scotland. This savoury roll is the Scottish equivalent of a croissant. Just who invented it has been lost in the mists of time but legend has it that the rowie has a local fisherman to thank for its origin.

A local seafarer asked his baker to make a bread roll that would be suitable for long trips in the North Sea. The baker took up the challenge and started off with a lump from his daily bread dough. To make a rowie that would keep, he added fat. The most readily available, and the least likely to toughen the rowie, was meat dripping from the butcher. The dripping was mixed with some dough to make it more pliable. He then rolled out some plain bread dough and covered it with the fatty-dripping dough. The mixture was then folded, rolled, kneaded and cut up into misshapen mounds. The baker then flattened the mixture into a large thin round shape and baked it in the oven for 40 minutes.

The crisp, crunchy rowie, with its faintly burnt saltiness, was hailed as a big success and soon every baker in the area was making it. The baking method has hardly altered since the 19th century but each baker alters the recipe slightly to account for local tastes. Texture and flavour varies wildly from baker to baker but Torry can boast one of the finest rowie exponents. Aitken's Bakery has been providing this local delicacy from its premises in Glenbervie Road since 1950. The current owners are the fourth generation to run this family-owned business.

Another local establishment, Low's Bakery, was a favourite stop for late night revellers in need of sustenance. Generations of Torry inhabitants, returning from a night on the town, had stopped off at Low's for a hot-out-of-the-oven rowie to help soak up the alcohol. Sadly, this establishment closed its doors for the last time in 2004.

Although Old Torry had its own post office long before the big expansion, Councillor James Pope identified the need for another one situated in the midst of the new sector. The new branch opened in Victoria Road in 1895. The first sub-postmaster was a Mr Paton who was succeeded a few years later by Mr Halley. The post office also had its own savings bank along with other useful facilities for the local residents.

Prior to 1891, Torry had been policed by Kincardineshire Constabulary but after the area's annexation it fell under the auspices of the Aberdeen force. A police sub-station was built in Victoria Road. The teak building was built to the same design as Glasgow's sub-stations. Inside there was room for several cells and accommodation for emergency equipment. The timber structure was eventually replaced in 1941 by a new stone construction. The old building was considered too small and unlikely to withstand a direct hit during an air raid.

In 1909, the Aberdeen City Police began to issue silver medals of merit to officers. The first of these was issued to Constable William Ritchie, an officer stationed at Torry. Ritchie was injured in the line of duty while apprehending a burglar in an incident in February of that year. Constable Ritchie heard the sound of breaking glass at the University Bar in Sinclair Road and went to investigate. He was too late to stop one man escaping but managed to grab his accomplice. The pair struggled for around fifteen minutes before Constable Ritchie finally managed to overpower his opponent and secure him with a rope.

Over the years the police have investigated many high profile cases centred on Torry. The area's most baffling crime began with a grim discovery in Greyhope Bay in December 1945. A severed limb was found washed ashore 100 yards east of St. Fittick's Road. Mutilation by a ship's propeller was swiftly discounted and forensics subsequently revealed that both a saw and a knife had removed the limb.

The preliminary examination revealed that the left forearm and hand was that of a young woman and that it had not been in the water long. Fortunately police were able to obtain fingerprints from the hand and quickly identify the victim as Elizabeth Ann Craig, who was better known as Betty Hadden. She had been arrested for several minor offences in the past and the police already had her fingerprints on file. The identification had been swift but the rest of the investigation would not go so smoothly.

Betty was just a few days short of her eighteenth birthday when she was murdered. The sullen brunette was a wayward and rebellious soul who had drifted in and out of employment since leaving school. Betty was well known in the seedy back street pubs and nightclubs of Aberdeen as a girl who was not averse to dodgy moneymaking practices.

Detectives were able to obtain more details of Betty's movements prior to her death. The last known sighting of her was on the evening before the limb was discovered washed up on Greyhope Bay. She had been seen talking to three sailors in Market Street.

The constabulary began a painstaking search of the foreshore between the Bay of Nigg and the River Don to try and uncover more clues. The harbour was dredged thoroughly until a strong tide forced the operation to be suspended. Also, an ingenious experiment was undertaken to ascertain where Betty's limb had been dumped in the water at sea or from the river estuary. The forelegs of pigs were dropped into the water at various points around the area to see where they would end up. From this they were able to deduce the limb had been thrown in from the Torry side. Whether the murder and dismemberment had taken place in Torry was still open to conjecture. However the investigation team began to concentrate their efforts in the area around Old Torry.

The murder squad began a door-to-door enquiry, promising to "go through Torry yard by yard". A map of the area was divided up into squares and a different sector was searched each day. This hunt brought some light relief to officers in an otherwise grim case. They reported that the house-proud ladies of Torry gave their abodes a good scrub-over on hearing of the impending visit from the law. Despite this extensive search no new evidence was uncovered and the investigation began to falter.

The force's next move smacked of desperation. The screams of a female had been heard in Torry around 2 a.m. on Wednesday 12th December. The shrieks, described as being made by a female in terror, were thought to have originated within the vicinity of Mansfield Road and Victoria Road. In an effort to gauge where the mystery screams came from, police enlisted the help of some female clerical staff. The females, accompanied by police officers, took it in turn to scream at different locations. By performing this bizarre ritual during the night, they hoped to illicit some response from Torry's sleeping population. The test failed miserably as not one person responded. As nobody came forward claiming to be the screaming woman it is now assumed that the original cries came from Betty.

It was strongly suspected that Betty had been murdered and mutilated in Torry, although no further evidence surfaced to support this theory. The rest of Betty's remains were never found and her arm was preserved in Aberdeen University's Anatomy Department. Sadly there was to be no justice for Betty Hadden. The police claimed to have a suspect but the trail gradually dried up. The enquiry was scaled down and eventually filed 'unsolved'.

During 1926, a comprehensive police box system was introduced which proved to be highly successful. In 1929 the scheme was expanded and Torry was allocated three units. The distinctive blue kiosks were erected at Baxter Street, Oscar Road and Victoria Road at the junction with South Esplanade West. The introduction of two-way radios spread rapidly throughout the 1960s and gradually the old police boxes were discarded in favour of the more modern telecommunication system.

Other emergency services were represented in Torry, albeit briefly. The fire station was situated just over the Victoria Bridge on South Esplanade East. It was opened at the end of the 19th century, alongside two other sub stations at Mile-End and Woodside. Inside a fireman was in constant attendance along with a cart, hose and ladders. Stations on the outskirts of the city were necessary as transport was not as quick as it is now. At the outbreak of a fire an appliance, complete with an experienced fireman, could be on the scene quickly. He would attend the fire until the main fire engine arrived from King Street. After the arrival of motor fire appliances, the brigade arrived more or less at the same time as the fireman from the sub station so eventually stations like the one in Torry were closed down.

An 8-acre area of land on the Girdleness headland was allocated for recreational purposes. Lord Provost James Walker opened Walker Park to the public in 1903. The Balnagask Golf Club opened on the 9th August 1905. A large crowd witnessed local M.P. Mr. J. W. Crombie perform the opening ceremony on the first tee. The people were then treated to an exhibition match between Archie Simpson and Arnaud Massy. Massy went on to win the 1907 Open Championship at Royal St. Georges.

The course was transformed from farmland in a mere four months and the greens were formed using turf from the grounds of Devanha House. The old clubhouse had a Tudor style look with pebble dashed walls and strips of wood at angles on the walls. There were wooden stairs outside at the rear of the building providing access to the changing rooms and lockers. It survived up to the 1950s, when it was demolished and replaced by a more modern structure. The course was highly popular with celebrities who were performing at HM Theatre and the Aberdeen Football Team had frequent outings there.

The Balnagask Golf Club was forced to close during both world wars as the land was requisitioned by the military. It remained as a private members club until 28th April 1955 and reopened as a municipal course three years later. The first members of the renamed Nigg Bay Golf Club teed off for the first time on 1st March 1958.

There were many other popular recreational facilities in the area. The Bay of Nigg was extremely popular with day-trippers, particularly between the war years. During the summer months tearooms provided refreshments while children were able to play on the swings and other amusements. A popular pastime at the Bay of Nigg was "buckie picking". Large crowds

Revellers enjoy the facilities at the Bay of Nigg.
© Aberdeen Library and Information Services

would frequently swarm to the area and gather up buckets full of buckies, or winkles.

The Torry inhabitants had another popular attraction virtually on their doorstep. The city's first "American Switchback" could be found just over the Victoria Bridge on North Esplanade West. Henry Duckworth built this primitive wooden roller coaster in 1886. The switchback's course, which consisted of a long straight line with just two dromedary style humps in between, would be considered quite tame in contrast to the death-defying attractions of today. Despite its simplistic design however, it became extremely popular and lasted through to 1911.

A roller-skating craze swept the country in the early part of the 20th century. Rinks sprouted up virtually everywhere and Torry was no exception. The Torry Skating Rink Syndicate opened their premises in Sinclair Road in 1909. However the skating craze began to fade shortly after and in an effort to bolster income they explored other avenues. They first showed films in 1910 and began regular cinema seasons during the winter. There were 2 shows each evening with 2 extra matinees on a Saturday. Dove

Paterson's Aberdeen Cinematograph Bureau supplied the films under the direction of general manager Robertson Prosser.

Films took over permanently on 2nd September 1912 and the rink became The Torry Picture Palace. The premises were extensively redecorated and the new management proudly proclaimed their establishment to be 'one of the cosiest picture halls in town'. Films were shown between 6 p.m. and 9 p.m. with tea and biscuit matinees every Wednesday. Tea dances were held regularly in the back hall after the evening's picture presentations had ended. Sadly though this burgeoning project was unable to survive the upheaval of World War One.

The housing programme was halted during the First World War. Afterwards the Government introduced legislation to alleviate the acute housing shortage. Aberdeen City Council took full advantage of the 1919 Housing Act, which offered generous funding to new housing projects. They proposed to build a mixture of housing on land owned by the City of Aberdeen Land Association.

The Garden City was developed as a series of concentric streets centred on Tullos Circle. The estate was a mixture of tenements and semi-detached houses. Certain streets were named after the hills of Deeside, which they overlooked - Morven, Brimmond and Battock. A suggestion that the streets be named after famous lochs was rejected after a fierce debate.

From the air the Garden City resembled a large wheel with Tullos Circle forming the hub. At the centre of Tullos Circle there was a raised area known by many as the "moundie". This circular mound was about 1.5 metres high and planted with shrubs. Pupils from the adjacent Torry Intermediate School were not allowed to play there until after the war when the shrubs were removed to make way for a recreational area.

This leafy suburb's homes were intended for the more affluent members of society. The electric lit, semi-detached homes were much desired at the time and echoed Lloyd George's ideology of "homes fit for heroes". The Town Clerk received several hundred applications from prospective tenants but priority was given to families of homeless ex-service men. The scheme was designed to avoid overcrowding with twelve homes built to an acre of ground and each tenant allocated from 200 to 300 yards of garden space. Rents were fixed between £25 and £35 depending on the type of house.

Building work on the first houses was completed in December 1920, despite delays caused by a joiners' strike. This dispute nearly endangered the project completely when a frustrated contractor threatened to remove his plant and machinery. It was only after the personal intervention of Mr Rust, the convenor of the housing committee, that a withdrawal was averted.

Many street names provide a clue to Torry's history. Menzies Road was named after the Menzies family of Pitfodels. Kirkhill Road is named after the hill the pilgrims descended to reach St. Fittick's Church, now named St. Fittick's Road. Abbey Road reminds us that the lands of Torry and Kincorth belonged to the Abbey of Arbroath. The Abbots are also responsible for another street name. They maintained a dovecot, fields and a summerhouse that overlooked the ford over the Dee. Eventually all that remained of the house was a ruined wall and Abbotswell Road is a corruption of the "Abbots Wall". Ladywell Place takes its name from the Lady Well, which stood east of St. Fittick's Kirk.

Oscar Road's name commemorates the disaster that befell the whaler 'Oscar' on the 1st April 1813. A full account of this incident appears elsewhere in this book. It is interesting to note that several well-known streets were originally known by a different name. Mansefield Road was previously called Corbie Well Road and Wood Street was earlier called Baker Street. Baxter Street was once Balnagask Road whilst Balnagask Road was formerly Torryhill Road. Polwarth Road follows the route of a farm track charmingly known to locals as the "Stinkin' Roadie".

Public transport in Torry was first provided in 1893. Torry successfully petitioned for a horse bus service, passenger fares being set at one penny with creels a penny extra. The service operated from Guild Street to avoid the steep ascent of Market Street. It was especially popular on public holidays when passengers went to the Bay of Nigg for picnics. The parish council made constant deputations to the Parliamentary Committee to

Looking down Sinclair Road towards Torry Harbour.
© Aberdeen Library and Information Services

persuade them that a tramway was necessary and eventually Aberdeen Corporation introduced the first tram to the area in 1903. Initially they only achieved limited success as the district lost out on the connecting link between Raik Road and George Street. However the Torry line was finally linked up with the main network via Bridge Street, a mirror being provided on the single-track at the foot to see around the corner.

The tram depot was a familiar landmark on the journey from Torry. It stood at the junction of North Esplanade West and Market Street. It was built around 1904 and was used for 7 years to house trams. Afterwards it was used as a paint shop for the trams before being used as storage facility by various firms. The Grade B listed building has recently been converted into offices and has undergone extensive conversions including the addition of a mezzanine floor and raised walkway inside the building. The outside retains its original pink and grey granite facade.

In 1913, the "Pay-as-you-Enter" system of fare collection was introduced to the Torry route. The No. 43 electric tram's route ran from Guild Street to St. Fittick's Road. However several complaints were received that other parts of Torry were poorly served by the service. This led to the introduction of buses in 1921. Tram passenger numbers virtually halved between the financial years 1919-20 and 1928-9. These routes had been unviable for many years and it became obvious to everyone that the tram's days were numbered.

The Torry service was finally withdrawn on Saturday, 28th February 1931. The tram made its final journey with several town councillors on board. The last trip happened during a blizzard and consequently very few people witnessed the event. The tramlines were removed from Victoria Bridge in August of that year but the ones in Victoria Road were not removed until 1978. They had been buried under the road after successive resurfacing work but weak parts in the road structure meant that they had to dig down to the original granite setts. The steel rails were eventually sold for scrap and the money used to help towards the cost of the road works.

The Torry Picture House in Crombie Road had provided entertainment for the locals since the early twenties. The "Torryers", as it was known, opened its doors on the 2nd May 1921. Lord Provost Sir James Taggart performed the opening ceremony. The management team behind the new venture were the same group responsible for the Torry Skating Rink before the war. They formed the company Torry Pictures Ltd, which was later renamed to Torry Cinemas Ltd.

The owners hired Edinburgh based architects Messrs Sutherland and George to begin the project in 1919. Two designs were drafted and the owners chose the more elaborate one. This second plan was lodged with the authorities in January 1920 and now incorporated a balcony instead of a raised area at the rear. The harled frontage consisted of two square towers situated either side of the main pitched roof auditorium. Above the main entrance was a large semi-circular window with a smaller circular window immediately above; two ordinary square windows flanked this arrangement.

The Cinema's original manager was J. H. Forrester and the first film shown was "The life of Christopher Columbus". Mr Harold Pollard provided musical accompaniment throughout the first performance. At this debut presentation cinemagoers could expect to pay between 5d and 1s. 6d, the

The Torry Cinema. © Aberdeen Library and Information Services

admission prices reflected the diverse social background of the community.

APP (Aberdeen Picture Palaces) took over the running of the premises by becoming a major shareholder on the first day of 1924. The cinema soon boasted its own house band led by Colin Nicol. By the end of the 1920s the band had expanded to 12 musicians with Herbert Jennings acting as musical director. The band accompanied the films with occasional dialogue provided by manager Edward Bell.

Occasionally variety artists appeared at the Torry Cinema. There is a record of a mind reader called L'Ada appearing there in 1922. Other attractions included a female impersonator and comedian Jack Gordon, brother of the better-known Harry. Musical entertainment was provided by Carnegie and MacDonald's Torry Jazz Band, Binky Morris and his band and the, rather bizarrely named, Hiawatha Japanese band. In November 1926, to cash in on the dance craze that was sweeping the nation at the time, the management ran a Charleston dancing competition. The winners and runners up received cash prizes of 15s and 10s respectively.

The Torry Cinema showed its first 'talkie' on Monday the 15th of September 1930. The first sound picture shown was 'The Trial Of Mary Duggan' starring Moira Shearer. The public's thirst for the new technology sounded the death knell of the silent film and within a relatively short space of time the cinema had dispensed with the house band's services.

APP became the sole owners of the cinema early in 1939 and promptly began an extensive refurbishment programme. These included a neon-lit canopy, a larger foyer and screen. A new Mirrophonic sound system was installed along with new curtains. The auditorium was tastefully decorated in panels of pale pink. However the planned re-opening had to be delayed because of the outbreak of the Second World War. For Torry filmgoers, the grandiose and opulent surroundings of the picture palace must have added a welcome touch of glamour to the otherwise bleak and austere conditions of wartime Britain.

The cinema was never a first run hall but its programme of Western, Romance and Detective films proved popular with the general public. During 1954, the cinema was altered to accommodate Cinemascope features. The screen was placed slightly forward reducing the size of the auditorium.

In the 1950s the popularity of television had an adverse affect on attendance numbers and profits began to freefall. The Cinema closed its doors on Saturday 2nd September 1966. The plan was for it to become a Bingo Hall and the equipment was shipped over from the Astoria. However a better offer for the site was accepted and the "Torryers" never reopened.

Torry had expanded well beyond its roots within a relatively short period of time. In 1947, the annual estimated valuation of Torry was £160,000. Its days of being an overlooked sleepy village were well and truly over and it had become an important area of Aberdeen. Despite being amalgamated into the city, Torry had assumed the character of a self-contained satellite town.

11
Education

Education in Torry can be traced back to the early 18th century. The Scottish Parliament decreed it was the duty of each parish to provide education for their children. Many parish councils reneged on this responsibility but Nigg parishioners embraced the idea and provided regular schooling in the area. The earliest mention of a schoolmaster happens in 1726 and there is evidence of at least 5 "dame schools" in the parish. These were establishments where older women taught the children for a small fee. The subjects taught were nothing more than the rudimentary three R's but consequently nearly everyone in the parish could read and write. In 1793 the schoolmaster was provided with a house and garden plus a basic salary of £8.33 depending on the range of subjects taught.

The Nigg Parish School was opened in 1849 at premises near the church. At the opening ceremony the teacher Mr Barnet announced that the children would be taught the principles of fishing, agriculture and cultivation as well as receiving a sound education.

School records for coastal communities constantly show the involvement of children in the fishing trade. The logbook from Nigg Parish School frequently shows that a number of the children were absent from the village during the herring fishing season. This is comparable to rural areas where children were withdrawn from school during the potato harvest. Fishing in the 19th century involved the whole family. Children were expected to help in various ways, for example, collecting bait for the lines and preparing fish for curing. Many of the older boys also went to sea with their fathers during the season and were often absent from school at this time.

Following the Scottish Education Act, and as the population grew, extra provision for schools had to be provided. Torry Public School was opened at Abbey Road on the 2nd May 1873 and on the first day 170 pupils registered. The roll reveals the first pupil to register was 10-year old William Wood, a fisherman's son. He eventually left the school after two and a half years, apparently to go to sea.

The first headmaster to be responsible for the school was William Yunnie. The building fund was boosted by a substantial donation of £1,400 by the fisherman's association. Seamanship and navigation were among the subjects taught at this time but they were ultimately dropped from the curriculum.

The school's roll is a fascinating document and reveals many fascinating facts about those early days. We learn that standard three had finished the repetition of Psalm 46 for the second time and that standard four had memorised the names of Scotland's mountains. During its first year in operation the school had to contend with an outbreak of scarlatina and at one point class numbers dwindled to just three pupils. Overcrowding was a severe problem and it was not uncommon for the schoolmaster to teach 100 pupils in a single room. Absenteeism was a fairly common occurrence in schools around the area. The seasonal demands of the fishing industry meant that children were often required to help out during busy periods.

Eventually the old school was extended and renamed Victoria Road Primary. The new part of the school was built in 1905 at a cost of £8,700. Various contractors carried out the work under the direction of J. A. O. Allan, the Aberdeen Education Board's architect. Part of the old school was incorporated in the new design and used to house the infant's section.

Victoria Road School has had a chequered history during wartime. It was occupied by troops during the First World War and was later bombed during World War II. During the night of 30th June 1940 over 100 incendiary bombs were dropped in the area and the school was the main casualty of this raid. The building was gutted by fire and sustained considerable damage.

A need for a second school was identified and architects Ellis and Wilson were hired to design it. Walker Road School was opened on the 8th March 1897. A sizeable amount of pupils transferred from Victoria Road with the remainder arriving from Marywell Street and Ferryhill Schools. Mr James Campbell was appointed as headmaster, he had previously filled a similar role at Frederick Street School. Later that month parents and local officials got an opportunity to view the school themselves at the official opening. The ceremony took place on Saturday 27th March.

During the First World War pupils attending Walker Road School often had to share their facilities with others. During August 1914. The ground floor was used as billeting quarters for troops awaiting deployment. Alternatively when the troops

Walker Road School.
© Aberdeen Library and Information Services

encamped at Victoria Road School the pupils were sent to share the facilities. Walker Road pupils attended classes in the morning while Victoria Road pupils attended in the afternoon.

The last intermediate pupils left the school when the school broke up for the summer vacation in 1926. A new school for intermediate pupils in the area was planned. Poverty and disease was rife in the area and this led to several problems for the school. In October 1932, the Medical Department made several surprise visits to the school. A number of pupils were excluded because of a lack of cleanliness. One of the main reasons cited for this was a lack of decent footwear and clothing for the pupils. An appeal to the parents led to clothing being distributed to needy pupils. During the early part of 1933 there were several outbreaks of influenza, chicken pox and mumps. Worst of all, there were 80 cases of scarlet fever and 20 cases of diphtheria.

There were extensive alterations to the school in 1934. Classrooms were altered to allow more space and light. Work on the new gym was completed in August of that year. School meals were first provided for 100 pupils on 19th May 1941 and at the end of the Second World War the school roll stood at 1,574 pupils.

In 1964, work began on construction of indoor toilet facilities. Work on this project was slow and took nearly a year to complete. In 1979 Mrs Jean Williams became the school's first Headmistress. Her successor Jeff Anderson was a former Walker Road pupil. In July 1981 several pupils from the outskirts of the catchment area were transferred to a new school at Loirston.

In the Walker Road School Centenary Booklet there is a set of guidelines that female members of staff had to adhere to. While not directly attributable to the school it is indicative of the general attitude to women in the profession in 1915.

1. *You may not marry during the term of your contract.*
2. *You are not to keep company with men.*
3. *You must be home between the hours of 8 p.m. and 6 a.m. unless attending a school function.*
4. *You may not loiter downtown in ice cream stores.*
5. *You may not travel beyond the city limits unless you have the permission of the chairman of the board.*
6. *You may not ride in a carriage or automobile with any man unless he is your father or brother.*
7. *You may not smoke cigarettes.*
8. *You may not dress in bright colours.*
9. *You may under no circumstances dye your hair.*
10. *You must wear at least two petticoats.*
11. *Your dresses must not be any shorter than two inches above the ankle.*
12. *To keep the school classroom neat and clean, you must sweep the floor at least once daily; scrub the floor at least once a week with hot, soapy water; clean the blackboards at least once a day; and start the fire at 7:00 a.m. so the room will be warm by 8:00 a.m.*

In 1937, Torry was chosen to be the first area in Aberdeen to get an experimental nursery school. Parents of pre-school age infants were offered the chance to send their children to the nursery in Oscar Road. This allowed mothers the freedom to go out to work if they wished. Sadly, after a long history spanning 68 years the nursery fell victim to falling pupil numbers and was deemed uneconomical to run. The nursery closed its doors for the final time on 1st July 2005 and the children were transferred to the three primary schools in the area

Torry Intermediate School was built on the brow of Torry Hill using the finest Peterhead Granite. Adam Birnie was the builder responsible for the project, which cost £25,000. The local education authority planned the school using typical Aberdeen prudence. It was built to serve the immediate requirements of the community with the option of extending the premises should it be required. The original building was all on one storey apart from the centre front section.

The first headmaster was Robert Bain who presided over 305 pupils and a staff of 12. When the school opened on 29th August 1927, the pupils had to sit on the floor for the first few weeks as no desks or seats had been provided. There were 12 classrooms, several specialist classrooms, a gymnasium and a meeting hall that held 525 people. Not all these facilities were available at first, as building work was not completed. The pupils only attended in the morning initially.

Unfinished building work was not the only problem the school had to deal with in its early years. The National Health Service was still two decades away and malnutrition and disease were common among pupils. The education authority took steps to reduce the number of these cases so supplies of shoes, spectacles and milk were provided cheaply. However during the depression money was scarce and many parents simply couldn't afford to buy the goods, even at the reduced rate.

After the war the school utilised the adjacent "Moundie" as a recreational facility. The Moundie was a raised circular mound of earth about the size of two football pitches. The area was surrounded by a large hedgerow and tall wire fence to prevent any stray balls from landing in the road. This was a popular playtime haunt for pupils as it was outside the main school boundary. Although it was fully supervised by staff it always instilled a greater sense of freedom amongst pupils. Playtime games and hi-jinks always seemed a lot better and rowdier in the "Moundie". Gradually more people moved into the area and the school leaving age was raised to 15 in 1947. This prompted the rear block to be expanded.

The school has been known at various times as Torry Intermediate, Torry Junior Secondary and Torry Secondary. In 1967 Aberdeen Education Committee decided to adopt the comprehensive system. The school changed its name once again to Torry Academy in 1970. This change to a secondary school allowed pupils to continue their education to Ordinary and Higher level and choose from a wider range of subjects.

Torry Intermediate adopted its school colours of dark blue, light blue and white and also introduced its own badge, designed by the pupils. They chose the Girdleness Lighthouse for the main motif. In 1960 The Lord Lyon King of Arms granted permission for Torry Secondary School to use its present badge, which was designed by one of the school's art teachers. The school motto "By Wisdom and Honesty" was also introduced at this time. This had been the motto of the Anderson family who owned the land where the school now stands.

The school roll continued to rise steadily throughout the 60s and 70s and the overcrowding began to adversely affect teaching levels. Several semi-permanent huts and portacabins were installed in the playgrounds and used as makeshift classrooms. It also became necessary to utilize the Old Aberdeen Academy building. First year pupils were ferried to and from Belmont Street using a daily shuttle bus service.

These measures were always intended as a temporary solution and eventually permission was granted for an extension at the front of the school. Sadly this meant that the mound was flattened to make way for the new block. The building work was eventually completed in 1977.

Construction of Tullos School began in 1938, but ceased during the Second World War. Building was resumed after the hostilities, and the school finally opened in 1950. The original plans were allowed to go ahead, and as a result the two-storey building was equipped with wide corridors and large classrooms that were ideal for the new teaching methods implemented after the war.

The school was designed by J A Ogg Allan and was intended as the principal civic building of the newly developing south Aberdeen. The sprawling low two-storey granite building with massive steel-framed windows gave the feeling of an open-air school. Separating the two wings was a tall glazed staircase with flagpole above at the point of change.

Following a round of budget cuts, Balnagask Infant School was amalgamated with Tullos Primary School, in 1982 and infant classes were housed in their own department. The ground floor was specially re-decorated and refurbished to house the new unit. Since then the nursery unit moved into rooms 3 and 4 of the main school. A support base of two rooms with an additional soft play area was established in 1997, providing 13 places for children who need extra support.

In 1999, Tullos successfully bid to become one of only two new community schools in the city. New teachers, trained in community education were appointed. As a result a range of agencies, including health promotions, social work, Barnardo's Outreach, police and community education all work alongside the teaching staff for the benefit of the pupils. This development placed the school in a unique position to provide educational opportunities from pre-school years to adult learning. In February 1993, the west wing of the school was up-graded at a cost of more than half a million pounds. Both the east wing and central area have been up-graded since then.

Torry was at the forefront of a new educational initiative when a revolutionary scheme called the Children's University was launched in November 2004. It was set up to reward young people for the time they spend in out-of-school hours learning activities. The initiative involved children from the feeder primary schools of Torry Academy - Tullos, Walker Road and Victoria Road.

The inaugural graduation ceremony was held in June 2005. Around 80 youngsters donned robes and gathered at Aberdeen University's Elphinstone

Hall venue where they were presented with their certificates. Guests were treated to a showing of films created by pupils as part of one of their modules. Walker Road's film focused on the Dee ferryboat disaster of 1876, and Victoria Road's short movie was set during World War II, entitled "It's An Air Raid".

The youngsters gathered credits for their learning hours and participated in a range of activities including chess, tree planting, filmmaking and a young investigators' club to encourage scientific interest.

Despite innovations like this, schools in the area face an uneasy future. Falling attendances have forced the education committee to undertake a review. One proposal is for the area to be served by just one "super school" with both primary and secondary pupils receiving their education in one establishment. There is a real possibility that certain schools in Torry could face closure.

12
Torry at War

We heard previously how Torry remained virtually unscathed during periods of conflict. Its relative isolation meant that it was virtually ignored by enemies who were far more interested in its larger neighbour. However that situation would change dramatically during the 20th century as advancements in military technology meant that even the most isolated areas of the country were within easy striking distance of the enemy. At the end of the 1800s, Torry had become an important area of Aberdeen. Its proximity to the harbour and its burgeoning maritime interests made it an important strategic target.

Aberdeen was one of the most frequently bombed cities in Scotland and suffered around 30 raids. Enemy bombers from Norway and Denmark carried out these brief attacks and a total of 178 people were killed as a result. The city was a recognised secondary target and fell victim mostly to what became known as 'tip and run' raids. If the aircraft failed to find their intended target they would fly over north east sites and dump their bombs.

The area experienced its first air attack on the 26th June 1940, when a bomber on a tip and run raid shed its load of high explosives on Home Farm

The remains of Victoria Road School after the Air Raid on 30th June 1940.
© Aberdeen Journals

at Nigg. The cottage was totally destroyed in the raid and the occupants, an elderly man and his daughter, were taken to hospital suffering from severe shock. Four bombs were dropped in total. The others destroyed a garage and damaged a crop of oats in a nearby field. Although the raid was no doubt distressing for those involved, the area affected was largely rural and areas of dense population were not affected. However Torry would not be so lucky next time.

Four days later at 11.45p.m, the sirens blew and the inhabitants of Torry experienced the first real blitz on the area. The bombers dropped their payload of incendiary bombs on Sinclair Road at the corner of Ferry Road and buildings on Abbey Road and Glenbervie Road sustained considerable damage. Fiddes' wood yard on Crombie Road fell victim to another bomb.

Several casualties were reported including Mr Robertson, the Minister of St. Peters Church, who was injured while helping to put out the fires. A bomb dropped outside the church and Mr Robertson rushed out and covered it with sand using a long handled shovel. In his haste however he inadvertently turned the bomb over and suffered burns to his hands. He was taken to a nearby first aid post for treatment.

Victoria Road was particularly badly hit with bombs landing in the vicinity of Baxter Street and Mansefield Road. 182 Victoria Road suffered a direct hit and an incendiary device burnt out Victoria Road School. The school, lined with pitch pine, was soon burning fiercely. The glare could be seen across the city and soon a crowd of onlookers gathered to witness the blaze, despite the danger of further attacks. The nearby sports pavilion was also damaged.

Torry was thankfully spared during the next two raids on the area. On the 13th August, high explosives were dropped 200 yards west of the Torry Battery entrance. No red alert was sounded during this raid and no serious damage to property was sustained. Later that month, on the 28th August 1940, a plane discarded its cargo harmlessly on the shore at the Bay of Nigg. The bomb craters can still be seen to this day at low tide.

The bombers returned with a vengeance on the 29th September. No siren

Wellington Road after the early morning raid on November 4th 1940.
© Aberdeen Journals

blast warned of the approaching menace and people were largely taken by surprise. One person died during the raid and five others were seriously injured. Property on Walker Road and Menzies Road were damaged by high explosives while the Co-operative buildings and Torry Library were also hit. Houses at 75/77 Oscar Road, 21/23 Grampian Road and 168 Oscar Road all received structural damage as a result of the attack. When a bomb fell on Oscar Road it left a crater the size of a double-decker bus in the middle of the street. The nearby nursery school also sustained damage.

Chaos reigned the following month when a single raider caused havoc during an early morning raid. The attack took place on November 4th 1940 just as people were getting ready for work. Harper's Engineering premises in Craigshaw were hit. The firm had changed its manufacturing process to help the war effort. They churned out tank turrets, shell casings and crankshafts for night fighters. Although the premises were damaged it didn't seriously affect the firm's output. Paterson's Sawmills in Wellington Road also sustained damage but tragedy struck when a bomb hit a block of flats.

Three people, including two brothers, were killed when a bomb landed in front of a block of flats in Wellington Road. The blast ripped the front of 55 Wellington Road apart and caused extensive damage to the surrounding properties. 45 people were injured as a result of the raid but others, including twins aged 4 months, had miraculous escapes. A family were in bed in a ground floor room yards from where the bomb landed. The explosion destroyed their home but the only injury sustained was a cut foot by one of the boys. The family crawled to safety from the rubble.

During the early hours of the 6th June 1941, four soldiers from the Royal Artillery, and one member of the Royal Engineers were killed when two bombs were dropped on the Torry Battery. Unfortunately there were also civilian casualties when two more high explosive devices fell in the vicinity. The first fell on Greyhope Cottages and virtually demolished them. The cottages were situated in front of the battery along from the breakwater and were used to house staff and their families. Miraculously, a couple and their eight-year-old daughter escaped with minor cuts and bruises. The second bomb destroyed a crane at the edge of the breakwater. A night watchman was killed and three other people were injured.

Enemy planes returned to Torry for the last time on the 8th of August 1941. Around midnight they dropped their consignment of high explosives onto Menzies Road and caused severe damage to several properties in the area. The force of the blast was so strong it caused windows to be blown in at neighbouring Walker Road.

There were several cases of good fortune. The raid destroyed an elderly woman's home but she was absent because she had been detained in hospital for a serious operation. She had been due home the previous night before but her release was postponed at the last minute. A five-year-old girl was saved by a picture, which fell from a wall and protected her from falling masonry. Two boats, The Elim and the Emulate, were sunk at their moorings in Torry Harbour; thankfully no crewmembers were on board at the time.

There was only one fatal casualty when a 16-year-old youth was killed while sheltering in a doorway. The bomb exploded 30 yards away from him and he died later in hospital from injuries sustained in the blast. Miraculously a man who had been standing next to him escaped with just a cut forehead.

Aberdeen experienced its worst night of bombing on 22nd April 1943. The raid left 128 people dead and hundreds more injured but Torry miraculously escaped unscathed. Many local people and historians have believed the German airmen were simply incompetent. However a very different story has been revealed to explain why Torry people had avoided the carnage.

Norman Beattie was manager of Aberdeen Harbour Board in 1960, when he visited Hamburg as part of a Board of Trade delegation. After the meeting, he was approached by a reporter from one of the German city's newspapers. The journalist asked if Norman remembered the raid on Aberdeen that April night 18 years before. Then the German asked if he knew why only the north part of the city was strafed.

The reporter told Norman his brother-in-law, Werner Bernstein, had been the pilot in command of that raid. He instructed all his pilots before they took off from Stavanger to restrict bombing to the area north of the Dee. It's alleged that Bernstein had married a Torry girl in March 1939 and he wanted to protect her family from the bombs.

There is no documentation in the Aberdeen Registrar's files of a Werner Bernstein marrying in Aberdeen immediately prior to the war. However the City Library records reveal the Luftwaffe Dornier bombers did fly out of Stavanger that night. This was believed to have been in retaliation for the recent massive RAF attack on Hamburg. Werner Bernstein was also believed to have drawn sketches of the bombing raid. These illustrations were published in the Berliner Zeitung magazine under the headline: The Way We Saw Aberdeen. Bernstein would certainly have kept his intentions quiet for fear of retaliation. So unless any further details can be unearthed, this story is liable to remain an enigma.

The Girdleness Lighthouse was slightly damaged in an explosion during the war but this was not due to an air raid. On the 18th November 1944 a mine drifted ashore and exploded. Luckily the damage was mainly confined to the doors and windows in the dwelling house and the tower.

What is often overlooked is the part played by local fishermen towards the war effort. They often experienced great danger while trawling in the North Sea and many lost their lives. 1941 was a particularly tragic year for vessels from Torry. In January the 'Oriole' A.305 struck a mine while fishing off the Faroe Islands. Two months later both the 'Kinclaven' A.17 and the 'Nisus' A.318 were attacked and sunk within days of each other. Another Torry great line vessel suffered a similar fate; the 'Fernbank' A.910 was lost during enemy action off Mygganaes, Faroe in November. In each case all crewmembers were killed.

In amongst the tragedy there were also tales of great heroism. Torry skipper Robert Buckett was awarded the MBE when his vessel successfully fought off a Nazi bomber's attack. John Bruce was decorated with the DSC for his role in the evacuation of Dunkirk and was later honoured with an MBE for destroying enemy aircraft while trawling from Aberdeen.

The Torry Battery played a vital role in protecting the north east coastline from enemy aggression and the installation was fully manned during both world wars. During both conflicts the gunners came from Wallasey in Cheshire. At the outbreak of the Second World War considerable improvements were made to protect the installation from air attacks. In 1943 a combined army and navy plotting room was built at the battery so that personnel could liase closely with the RAF squadrons at Dyce. Searchlights and anti-aircraft guns were installed, while concrete overhead covers were built to protect the guns from dive-bombers. Two Royal Navy guns were placed alongside Girdleness Lighthouse and three howitzers were installed at the battery.

A friendly fire tragedy was narrowly averted in 1941. Two unidentified vessels were seen approaching the harbour on the 3rd June. The order was given to fire at them and then swiftly countermanded when it was established that these ships were British. Two shells were fired but thankfully they missed. A month later the machine guns were fired in earnest at an enemy plane that had dropped bombs off Kinnaird Head. The plane was eventually shot down at St Cyrus.

Anti-tank blocks were laid at various points at Nigg Bay and Cove to help defend the coastline. These blocks of reinforced concrete were made at the location they were to be used. Their purpose was to block or impede the progress of tanks. If a tank attempted to cross them it would expose its vulnerable underside to fire. An example of one of these blocks still exists today at Cove.

An anti-aircraft gun emplacement based at Peterseat on Tullos Hill supplemented the coastal defences. The location was established around 1941 with four static guns in place, that figure had risen to eight by the end of the war. Five of the gun emplacements were arranged in an arc around the command post with another three situated in an adjacent field. Each gun was set on to a concrete foundation built into a circular pit.

The camp contained several Nissen huts used for administrative and accommodation purposes. The sunken command post contained assorted instruments to target enemy aircraft. The command post employed many women as predictors and plotters who collated information about incoming enemy planes. The predictor worked on the roof of the command post. The sides of the building were protected behind piles of earth, but the people on the roof were fairly unprotected. Various Royal Artillery teams manned the site apart for a brief period at the end of 1943. The City of Aberdeen Home Guard occupied Peterseat Camp from October to December of that year.

The site was later used as a hostel for prisoners of war. Between 1945 and 1948 German and Italian prisoners were moved from POW Camp 75 at Laurencekirk to await repatriation. The inmates wore khaki uniforms with big yellow patches sewn on. They became a familiar site around Torry as they attended their work details.

By all accounts, relations between the prisoners and the locals were convivial. The detainees even had their own football team and played matches against local amateur teams on a pitch sited within the camp's grounds. At first the POW camp was fenced with barbed wire and protected by some military guards. Later there was just a simple wire fence to keep out undesired visitors, such as stray ladies from the town. Initially the military authorities undertook two daily roll calls but this was later reduced to just one.

Officially the prisoners were not allowed money but they earned some pay by working on farms and doing odd jobs around the area. Some of the Italians were used as labourers in Fiddes' wood yard. Until July 1947 prisoners were given 6 shillings for a 48-hour working week, afterwards this figure rose to 9 shillings per week.

Each Nissen hut housed 15 to 18 prisoners. Inside there were wooden double-decker beds with straw filled mattresses. Each prisoner was supplied with two blankets. Heating was provided by one coal stove. There was also a bathroom hut where the prisoners were allowed hot water on Saturdays for their weekly shower. Religious prisoners were allowed to attend church on Sundays. Every week they were marched over to Nigg Kirk where several pews were reserved for them.

On VE day some over-enthusiastic schoolchildren lit a bonfire in celebration. The fire quickly went out of control and spread across Tullos Hill. As firemen battled to control the fire, the flames came perilously close to engulfing the camp. Although the prisoners were in no immediate danger they were allowed out to help beat out the fire.

I haven't been able to ascertain exactly when the camp was closed but there were still prisoners in the camp waiting to be repatriated in 1946. When the site was abandoned the buildings and installations were carefully dismantled and removed. The gun emplacements were blown up and part of the land was reclaimed for agriculture.

Little remains of the camp now except for a couple of concrete bases. In January 2001 an archaeological investigation was carried out at the site. The remains of three gun emplacements were found. As a result of this excavation several people who had memories of Peterseat came forward, including one elderly gentleman from Germany who had been a prisoner there during the war.

After the war a major rebuilding scheme was undertaken. The demand for housing was far outstripping the supply so the Government stepped in with a solution. 1,500 temporary houses in the form of pre-fabricated bungalows were supplied to Aberdeen Council. Several streets of these 'Prefabs', as they became known, were erected at Tullos in 1948. Although they were only meant to be temporary, these kit houses lasted a lot longer than expected. The prefabs were planned to last for around a decade but existed until the late 1970s. Incredibly at the time of their demise the architect's department examined the feasibility of extending their life for another 10 years but eventually they recommended the area be used for industrial development.

Most tenants remember the houses fondly but perhaps they are looking at them through rose-tinted spectacles. The prefabs were cold in the winter and the aluminium frame was prone to erosion and used to shudder if a lorry drove past. The last remaining examples of the Prefabs on Wellington Road were demolished in 1979.

13
New Torry

Following the war, a need for housing prompted another expansion in Torry's boundaries. A sizeable amount of private land was sold to the council after the Second World War. The Balnagask Estate stretched from the golf course to the fields that overlooked both the Bay of Nigg and the railway line. Two farms straddled the land - Kirkhill Farm was situated on the left side of the hill and Home Farm located on land now occupied by Baxter Court. The estate also included an area of land around Balnagask Road and the top of Baxter Street.

The Davidson family had occupied Balnagask House since the mid 19th century. Colonel Davidson spent his army career in India before returning home after retiring from the Hussars. The Colonel was a stern man with a neat trimmed beard, who ran the estate with military precision. He struck an imposing figure as he strode around the estate dressed in his tweeds. The Colonel died in 1932 and his wife died 8 years later. The Colonel's funeral was a big event that attracted a large number of spectators. The service was held in St Andrew's Cathedral, King Street then the cortege with several cars led the procession to St. Fittick's Churchyard via Victoria Road. The couple are buried in a fenced off section on the left as you walk on the path to the church.

The couple's son Alistair was a bit of a ladies man by all accounts. He was a Captain in the Territorial Army, despite suffering from ill health. The land was sold to the council when the Captain died in 1949 and converted to an old folks home in 1950. Some elderly inhabitants of Torry continue to benefit from the legacy as sheltered housing now stands on the site of Balnagask House.

The farm settlements on the south side of Torry Hill had survived Torry's rapid expansion at the end of the 19th century but their time was running out. A map, dated 1868, showed several farms scattered along the vale of Tullos. Craiginches Farm was located on the site now occupied by Girdleness

Terrace. Tullos House stood on the northern slopes of Torry Hill near to Nigg Kirk. Middleton Farm, later known as 'Millie's Farm' was situated further west on the edge of what is now the Tullos Industrial Estate. Its nearest neighbour 'North Middleton' was sited in the vicinity of where Tullos School now stands. None of these farms made it into the 21st century.

Permission was eventually given for houses to be built on the southern slopes of Torry hill. More houses were built on Balnagask Road and Wellington Road. With the addition of the housing scheme centred on Kirkhill Road it eventually encompassed an area as far as the main railway line.

As a result of the downturn in the fishing industry, the council were actively looking to attract new businesses and industries to the area. Several areas were earmarked for industrial development and once again Torry's strategic importance was recognised. Its proximity to the harbour and main route south made it an ideal candidate for development.

The Tullos industrial estate stretched between the area south of the railway line and Kincorth. The first company to settle in the area was Trollope and Colls Ltd. The company opened their concrete pipeworks in 1936. Two years later Aberdeen City Town Council bought the Tullos estate at a cost of £13,000. Sir Stafford Cripps opened a Ministry of Aircraft factory on the site in 1944. After the war the factory was taken over by Tullos Ltd. to manufacture agricultural machinery.

The Board of Trade set up a couple of advance factories and over the next decade the industrial estate expanded. The cheap rates and subsidies attracted many firms and every available site was quickly occupied. A familiar Torry landmark sprouted up at this time. The Gasometer stood on the site next to the Consolidated Pneumatic Tools factory and remained there until the late 1980s. It was then partly demolished and now only the base remains, much to the delight of local seagulls who use it as a nesting area.

The oil boom of the 1970s ushered in a new era of prosperity for Torry. The trawlers that once occupied Torry Dock were gradually replaced with oil supply vessels. The urgent need for premises prompted another expansion to the Tullos Industrial Estate and an area to the east, occupied by 'Millie's fairm' was swallowed up. The last available piece of green belt was eventually bought and the industrial estate spread up the slopes towards Cove. A large part of this area became the headquarters for Shell UK.

Sadly Tullos Hill was to be a victim of urban redevelopment and a large part of it has disappeared over the past 30 years. A large swathe of trees on the northern slopes of Tullos Hill were cut down in the early 1970s to facilitate access to a landfill site which blighted the scenery for nearly two decades. The site, which was run by Aberdeen Council, has now been closed down but another eyesore has sprung up to take its place. A sewage treatment plant has been built on ground overlooking the Bay of Nigg.

The urban sprawl of Torry and the incessant encroachment of the Altens Industrial Estate have led to concerns over the future of this area. However the planned re-establishment of Tullos Hill as a recreation area with trees and paths should go some way to allaying these fears. Gorse and broom still covers much of the expanse, and deer, foxes and small birds of prey are occasionally spotted.

Erosion at Nigg Bay continues to be a problem. In 1968 Aberdeen Corporation placed large amounts of rubble into the sea to prevent erosion close to the foot of the cliffs. The buffer zone between the cliffs and the sea would have been around 45m but years of storm erosion in the bay has removed around 15 to 20m of defences. It is highly likely there will be a need for new defences at this site in the not too distant future.

Other areas of Torry have also evolved considerably from their humble origins. It's hard to believe that just over a century ago the beautiful Vale of Tullos was once a thriving agricultural area with farm settlements stretching from Nigg Bay to the River Dee. The scene is very different today and one our forefathers would scarcely believe. The area south of the railway line is full of car showrooms, oil yards and waste recycling plants. Northwards, a vast area of densely packed housing covers the hillside.

This constant development would necessitate the return of one of the emergency services to the area for the first time in eighty years. In the early

1980s with the rapid expansion to Aberdeen through oil and its related industries, it was decided that the fire cover for the city would need to be upgraded to cope with increasing industrial development to the south of the city.

Souterhead Road in the Altens district of Aberdeen was picked as the site for the first new full time fire station to be opened since 1968. Plans for the construction were drawn up by W. S. Scott, RIBA, ARAS, Director of Architectural Services for the Grampian Region, working in liaison with the local fire authority to determine the needs of a present day fire service. The project cost £606,000 to complete.

A.D.O. Coutts, the Station Commander, and 'B' Watch manned the station on the 6th December 1982. They didn't have to wait long for the first callout, that day in fact, when Station Officer Rennie and his crew attended an incident in Torry. The official opening date for Station 97 - Altens is given as the 7th February, 1983, when it was officially opened by Councillor J. A. S. MacPherson C.B.E., Chairman of the Public Protection Committee for the region.

After the war the great demand for housing was addressed by the council. After 1959, Aberdeen City Council's Housing Committee built multi-storey blocks in the suburbs, and larger 'slab' blocks on slum clearance sites. By 1971, public authorities owned almost half of Aberdeen's housing, nearly a third of which had been built since 1952.

In the 1960s, Aberdeen City council gave the go ahead for a large housing estate to be built at Balnagask. The new estate began to swallow up acres of land on the southern slopes of Torry Hill as the new cuboid shaped houses enveloped the elegant villas of Balnagask. The box shaped homes affectionately known as 'The Hen Hooses' by residents differed wildly to the regimented ideas of past town planners. The homes sprawled over a large area bordered by Balnagask Road in the north, Girdleness Road in the west and St. Fittick's Road in the east. The first phase of the housing scheme was completed in 1967 and consisted mostly of two-storey terraced flats.

The second phase commenced in 1968. The Housing Committee of

Balnagask Housing Scheme under construction © Aberdeen Journals.

Aberdeen Corporation built a number of five-storey blocks of flats. They had flat roofs, recessed balconies and were clad in granite aggregate blockwork. This was introduced when granite became too expensive to use. Blocks made from waste stone, or panels set with rubble from demolished buildings were used in many council developments. The flats formed part of a larger development that included three tower blocks. The skyscraper had 14 storeys and contained 156 flats in total. Grampian, Brimmond and Morven Courts offered a commanding view over the Bay of Nigg.

At one point a third phase was planned for the scheme to be extended as far as the railway line. However this was rejected because of soggy ground, much to the delight of local ornithologists. The marsh had been home to many species of birds such as snipe, mallard and the lapwing. Sadly the birds have long since disappeared. In common with other familiar inhabitants and landmarks of Torry, such as the skating rink, the Old Torry fisherman and the ferry across the Dee, they are fast becoming a vague memory of times past.

Sadly in recent years the number of retailers has continued to fall. The once busy shopping centre of Victoria Road is a pale imitation of its former self.

In the past most people did not have the benefit of freezers to store food in and so used to patronise the local shops more frequently each week. The average household now has two cars at its disposal and it is far easier to make a weekly shopping trip to the hypermarkets on the outskirts of town.

In recent years Torry has had more than its fair share of problems caused by urban deprivation. The area has a higher proportion of unemployed people than in other parts of the city. The unemployment rate currently stands at 3%. Statistics show there is a substantial drugs problem in Torry and the number of general health problems is also higher than elsewhere. In spite of this, Torry still somehow manages to retain its community spirit.

Torry is highlighted as a priority area for Aberdeen's Community Regeneration Strategy. Both the council and local community groups are constantly working to improve the situation and it seems their efforts are beginning to pay off. These projects included the building of a sports and community neighbourhood centre in Oscar Road. The arrival of the Torry Neighbourhood Centre means for the first time all Torry residents are able to access primary health care, community police services and social work in one place.

The average property sale in 2004 was £34,000, compared to £91,000 in the Aberdeen City area. Torry's reputation for cheap housing has traditionally attracted students. However more recently economic migrants from Eastern Europe, Poland in particular, have moved into the area. In June 2006, a Polish shop opened in Victoria Road to cater for the sizeable Polish community.

In the last 150 years, Torry has evolved from its origins as a little fishing village to become part of a vibrant city. Its fate is intrinsically linked to the fortunes of Aberdeen. The area has undoubtedly prospered economically due to its incorporation within the city boundaries and Torry is now well and truly just another city suburb. Despite this, Torry has managed somehow to retain its identity and the independent spirit so prevalent amongst its past residents has continued to this day. The "loons" and "quines" of the area are immensely proud of their local heritage and will continue to ensure that Torry remains a vital part of Aberdeen for many years to come.

14
Bibliography

Craiginches Prison - Scottish Prison Services www.sps.gov.uk
Aberdeen - Its Traditions and History - William Robbie 1893
Torry - James Spence MA
Living the Fishing - Paul Thomson, with Tony Wailey and
Trevor Lummis - 1983
Torry Times 1 - Torry Oral History Group - Aberdeen City Council 2001
Torry Times 2 - Torry Oral History Group - Aberdeen City Council 2003
The North East of Scotland Survey - 1963
The Port of Aberdeen - Victoria Clark 1922
City by the Grey North Sea - Fenton Wyness - 1965
The Balnagask Headland and Bay of Nigg - Peter Robinson 2005
The Real Price of Fish, Aberdeen Steam Trawler Losses 1887-1961
 - George F. Ritchie 1991
Aberdeen and the Fishing Industry in the 1870s - J. J. Waterman
21 Aberdeen Events of the 19th Century - John A Henderson 1912
Torry Battery - Anne Johnstone Aberdeen Arts and Recreation Division
Aberdeen - Ottakar's Local History Series - Graham Crowe 2002
Shipwrecks Of North East Scotland 1444-1990
- David M Ferguson 1991
Aul Torry O' Fish and Fowk - David Atherton 1992
Aberdeen of Old - Edward Meldrum
History of the Scottish Regiments - William Pratt Paul 1959
Far wis ye fin the siren blew? - David Atherton 1993
Aberdeen Before 1800, A New History - E. Patricia Dennison,
David Ditchburn and Michael Lynch
Aberdeen 1800 - 2000, A New History - W. Hamish Fraser and Clive H.
Lee
Torry Past to Present 1495 - 1995 - George Wood
Scottish Bodysnatchers - Norman Adams 2002
The Diced Cap - The Story of Aberdeen City Police - Introduction by
Fenton Wyness 1972

Aberdeen an Illustrated Architecture Guide - W. A. Brogden 1986
Torry Battery - A Neglected Treasure - Gordon Bathgate 2002
Bygone Days of Footdee - Andrew Baxter
The Book of St. Fittick - Thomas White Ogilvie 1901
Aberdeen - Images of Scotland - Alistair Burnett 1999
Silver Screen in the Silver City - History of Cinemas in Aberdeen 1896 - 1987 - Michael Thomson
From Fisherfolk to Torryfolk - Colin A Milne
A Thousand Years of Aberdeen - Alexander Keith MA. LL. B. 1972
Rise and Progress of the Granite Industry in Aberdeen - William Diack
Torry Academy Commemorative Booklet 1927 - 1977 - Mary Loggie
Aberdeen at War - Paul Harris - 1987
Aberdeen in the 19th Century The Making of the Modern City - John S Smith & David Stevenson 1988
Auld Torry - An Epitaph - Donald Smith 1973
Aberdeen In Bygone Days - Robert Anderson 1910
Walker Road School Centenary Booklet - 1996
Blood and Granite - Norman Adams 2003
Aberdeen Harbour - The Taming of the Dee - John S Smith - 1988

An aerial view of Torry © Aberdeen Journals.

Torry Battery 150 Years of History - Aberdeen City Council 2004

History of New and Old Torry - Alex Ledingham 1903

Nigg Bay - A Short Guide - McDonald and Philip 1923

Peterseat Ack Ack Battery and POW Camp - Alison Cameron - Aberdeen City Council

Granite City- History of Aberdeen - Robert Smith 2002

Aberdonia: Footdee in the Last Century - Anne Dundas Alladyce 1843

Aberdeen of Auld Lang Syne - Charles A Wilson 1948

The Hidden City - The Story of Aberdeen and Its People - Robert Smith 2004

When home was the Torry Battery – Chris Croly 2006

Memories Of Wartime Aberdeen - Arthur Binnie 2006

Maritime Aberdeen - John Edwards 2004

Aberdeen Curiosities - Robert Smith 1997

Acknowledgements

My sincere thanks to the following people whose help and encouragement during the writing of this book was greatly appreciated.

Alison Cameron & Chris Croly - *Archaeology Department, Aberdeen City Council*
John Main and Bruce Noble - *Old Torry Heritage Society*
Susan Bell and Catherine Taylor - *Aberdeen Central Library*
John Edwards - *Aberdeen Maritime Museum*
David Wilson - *Langstane Press*
Donald Martin and Charles Allan - *Aberdeen Journals Limited.*